BT 613 .M3613 1992
Margerie, Bertrand de.
 Heart of Mary, heart of the Church : a
theological synthesis

HEART OF MARY
HEART OF THE CHURCH

By the Same Author

Le Coeur de Marie, Coeur de l'Église, Paris, Lethielleux, 1967.

Le Christ pour le Monde, Beauchesne, Paris, 1971; Prix Montyon de l'Académie française, 1971; mentionné par Paul VI (*Oss. Rom.*, 30 mars 1972).

Reinhold Niebuhr, théologien de la communauté mondiale, Paris, DDB, 1969, coll. Musaeum Lessianum.

La Trinité chrétienne dans l'historie, Paris, Beauchesne, 1975, coll. «Bibl. de théol. historique», vol. n° 31.

Sacrements et développement intégral, Paris, Téqui, 1977; Prix Trubert de l'Académie française, 1978.

Les Divorcés remariés face à l'Eucharistie, Paris, Téqui, 1979.

Vers la plénitude de la Communion, Paris, Téqui, 1980.

Retraite théologique, Résiac, 53150 Montsûrs, Mayenne, France, 1981.

Les Perfections du Dieu de Jésus-Christ, Paris, Cerf, 1981.

S'ouvir à la Miséricorde. Le Sacrement de pénitence, Paris, Fac, 1982. En collaboration avec P. Toinet.

Introduction à l'Historie de l'Exégès:
I.   *Les Pères grecs et orientaux,* Paris, Cerf, 1980.
II. *Les Premiers Grands Exégètes latins,* Paris, Cerf, 1983.
III. *Saint Augustin,* Prix Montyon 1984 de l'Académie française.
IV. *De saint Léon le Grand à saint Bernard,* 1990.

Communion quotidienne et confession fréquente, Résiac, B.P. 6, 53150 Montsûrs, Mayenne, France, 1987.

Faites ceci en Mémorial de Moi: Bellarmin (Montréal) et Beauchesne, Paris, 1989.

In English

Christ for the World, Chicago, Franciscan Herald Press, 1974.

Sacraments and Social Progress, Chicago, Franciscan Herald Press, 1974.

Theological Retreat, Chicago, Franciscan Herald Press, 1977.

Remarried Divorcees and Eucharistic Communion, Boston, Daughters of St. Paul, 1980.

Human Knowledge of Jesus, Boston, Daughters of St. Paul, 1981.

HEART OF MARY
HEART OF THE CHURCH

A Theological Synthesis

Bertrand de Margerie, S.J.

Translated by
Sr. Mary Thomas Noble, O.P.

AMI Press
Washington, New Jersey

Title of the French original
LE COEUR DE MARIE
COEUR DE L'ÉGLISE
ESSAI DE SYNTHÈSE THÉOLOGIQUE
© 1967, Editions P. Lethielleux
Paris

Imprimi potest: Rev. Joseph P. Parkes, S.J.
Provincial
New York Province
Society of Jesus
September 20, 1991

In accord with Canon 827 of the New Code of Canon Law, this publication has been submitted to a censor of the Diocese and nothing being found contrary to faith and morals we hereby grant permission in accord with Canon 824 that it be published.

Rev. Msgr. John B. Szymanski
Vicar General
Diocese of Metuchen
October 15, 1991

N.B. The imprimatur implies nothing more than the material contained in the publication has been examined by diocesan censors and nothing contrary to faith and morals has been found therein.

Cover art — The cover features an image of the Immaculate Heart of Mary from the icon *The Apparition of the Mother of God at Fatima* by Terence J. Nelson. The Virgin's hands are extended in the ancient manner of intercession, demonstrating her maternal concern for her spiritual children. Her Immaculate Heart surrounded by thorns draws our attention to her request for the First Saturday Devotion of reparation.

Printed in the United States of America

Library of Congress Catalogue Card No: 92-85103

ISBN 0-56036-041-0

Contents

APPENDIX

MARIAN SUGGESTIONS FOR THE REFORM
OF THE LATIN RITE CALENDAR

Preface

The Blessed Virgin Mary's relationship to the Church is much more important and foundational than many Catholics realize. Mary is, in fact, the first and pre-eminent member of the Church. In a certain sense, the Church actually began at the moment of her Immaculate Conception. Blessed Benedicta of the Cross, Edith Stein, the famous philosopher, spiritual writer and martyr of Carmel, sought to comprehend this beautiful truth: "The original cell of all redeemed mankind is Mary, in whom first took place the purification and sanctification through Christ and impregnation by the Holy Spirit. Before the Son of Man was born of the Virgin, the Son of God conceived of this very virgin as one full of grace and He created the Church in her and with her."

Mary, the first to believe in Christ and make a place for Him in the world, is not only the model of faith, hope and charity for every Christian but is also the personification of the Church — the image and model of the Church — as the Virgin-Spouse "holy and immaculate, without stain or wrinkle" (Eph. 5:27). The experience of saints and sinners proves the following to be true: The more the person of faith penetrates the riches of Mary, the more he or she will appreciate the Church, indissolubly wed to the Holy Spirit, as a mystery of faith that eludes the comprehension of mere human reason.

As Mary is *semper virgo*, so the Church as the universal body of pastors and faithful, is virginal in her uncompromising adherence to the faith revealed by Jesus Christ. The Church, like Mary, is Bride in the loving surrender of her members to the Divine Bridegroom. In every celebration of the Holy Eucharist this mutual surrender is realized. "Two" become one flesh as heaven unites with earth in the Son's hymn of praise of the Father. In union with Mary, Mother of God and all of God's children, the Church generates and nurtures the life of Jesus in the souls of the members of our fallen race.

It is indeed true to say that the more a person understands Mary, the more he or she will appreciate the deep, inner mystery of the Church. Fr. Bertrand de Margerie S.J. is a devoted and very learned son of the Blesed Virgin. In his work, *Heart of Mary, Heart of the Church*, he seeks to lead us deeper into the heart of the Mother of God so that we may stand in awe before the maternal heart of the Church.

The World Apostolate of Fatima is delighted to present Father de Margerie's brilliant work during the seventy-fifth anniversary celebration of the apparitions of Our Blessed Mother at Fatima. The propagation of devotion to Mary's Immaculate Heart is the primary goal of the Fatima Apostolate. I am certain that Father de Margerie's profound reflections on the Immaculate Virgin's relationship to the Church will advance this purpose and lead many to know, love and serve Jesus Christ in the mysterious and mystical communion of the Church, whose heart is ever virginal, bridal and maternal.

Rev. Frederick L. Miller, S.T.D.
Shrine of the Immaculate Heart of Mary
Washington, New Jersey
October 13, 1992

Author's Preface

This short work on the heart of Mary attempts to link a subject dear to many Catholics, particularly to the pilgrims of Fatima, with the understanding, shared by a good number of Russian Orthodox and Latin theologians, of the mission of Mary in the Church: to be the heart of the Mystical Body of Christ.

This linkage is considered in the context of each of the events and states of life in which the holiness of Mary has been manifested and developed: virgin, wife, mother and widow.

They are contemplated in the light of Tradition (apostolic and ecclesial), Scripture and the Magisterium. Particular attention is given to the abundant teachings of Popes Pius XII and John Paul II and the Second Vatican Council.

The author, a member of the American and French Mariological societies, has had recourse to the rich works of the international Marian congresses, many of which he has attended, and to the different liturgies of the Church, both in the East and West.

It is the author's hope that *Heart of Mary, Heart of the Church* will deepen the reader's knowledge both of the Church and of Mary. Without the Church, we would not know Mary; without a knowledge of Mary, our understanding of the mystery of the Church is incomplete.

Introduction

The Soundless Depths of Her Mystery

The Dogmatic Constitution *Lumen Gentium* makes it very clear that the Catholic Church never wearies — and doubtless never will — of fixing a child's gaze upon the glorious face of its mother, of sounding the soundless depths of her mystery of love. If Mary is, as a Byzantine chant puts it, "a depth which the eyes of angels cannot fathom and a height beyond the reach of human reason," obviously she ought always to be the object of the Church's contemplation, stimulating theologians to ever fresh reflection.

We find in the mystery of Mary a unique and felicitous expression of the eternal love of the Divine Persons for men and angels, and of Christ's love for his Church.

In the economy of redemption all of Mary's mysteries, states, actions and words, all of her free decisions and privileges[1] express the ardent love of her pierced and glorious heart. This love is directed to God, the angels, to all

---

1. St. Robert Bellarmine explains that the Virgin's free will concurred in several of her privileges (*Opera oratoria postuma,* Gregorian University, Rome, Vol. II, pp. 87-88). It would obviously be difficult to apply this to the Immaculate Conception, and yet, from the first instant of her existence, Mary's freedom was sanctified by infused charity.

humanity and to the Church of which she is at once member and mother. Her love is, in the order of creation, the most perfect reflection of Uncreated Love.

In this synthesis I propose to contemplate the whole mystery of Mary from the viewpoint of her heart and its ecclesial radiation. Perhaps in this way I may bring to greater fruitfulness Scheeben's remarkable intuitions in the last century:

"Mary's heart is the vital center of her person. Since the heart is the organ of physical, as well as spiritual maternity, Mary's heart symbolizes her in her personal character of mother. Her entire being and activity are caught up, subsumed in the concept of the mystical heart of the Mystical Body of Christ."[2]

In our century the Russian Orthodox theologian V. Iljin was responding, doubtless unconsciously, to Scheeben when he expressed the ecclesial thrust of his personal faith in the Immaculate Conception:

"Mary is the heart of the Church. In the confession of her radical, pristine purity, that is to say her integrity, her 'tselomoudriia' (chastity and also highest wisdom) we find a witness to the Church's unity. This unity may be viewed as something already realized, and also as something to be realized, externally and empirically, with the entrance of the

---

2. Scheeben, *La Mere virginale du Sauveur*, Desclee de Brouwer, Bruges, 1953, pp. 208-9. We note, however, that "it is as a symbol of love, and not as an organ of love, that the devotion (to the heart of Jesus) has been approved and has made its way" (J. Bainvel, *Dictionnaire de Theologie Cath.*, art. Coeur Sacre de Jesus, Vol. III, Part I, col. 296). Bainvel adds (ibid., col. 297) this evidence of Claude Bernard: "The heart, the principal organ for the circulation of the blood, is also a center for all sensitive nervous impressions....The love which makes the heart throb is not merely a poetic expression, it is also a psychological reality." This testimony of a celebrated sage is particularly enlightening.

full, predetermined number of the elect into the Church. At the time preordained by the Father's power, the Mother of God, in the strength of the indwelling Holy Spirit, will bring forth the plenitude of the elect."[3]

In Part One, Mary's heart will be considered as it is seen in dogmatic teaching and in Marian devotion: the maternal heart of the Church. Here I shall draw from the inexhaustible sources of Scripture and the Fathers, and follow the lead of the Magisterium, whose privilege it is to express this truth in the liturgy. Part Two will deal more particularly with certain theological problems, as well as some ecumenical and pastoral advantages arising from the following affirmation: the Immaculate Heart of Mary is the heart and noblest member of the Mystical Body of Christ.

---

3. Iljin, *Rousskj katoliceskij Vestnik* (1951), No. 4, p. 220. Perhaps inadvertently, Iljin was applying a principle of the theology of the relationship between Mary and the Church: "All that the Church receives already exists, in its plenitude and perfect purity, in Mary."

PART I

The Heart of Mary
And
The Insights of Mariology

The Concept of the Heart of Mary

When we speak of "the heart of Mary," we mean the Holy Virgin's physical heart of flesh. This is the symbol of her twofold love, spiritual and affective, for God and mankind; it is also the symbol of all the virtues, acquired and infused, and all the charisms and gifts of the Mother of God. (See chapter 9.)

"The heart of Mary" therefore expresses and symbolizes a love that is at once created, redeemed and co-redeeming; human and supernatural; immaculate, virginal, nuptial,[4] maternal and glorified in the sight of the Divine Persons, angels and men. Following Scheeben, who in turn draws his inspiration from St. Thomas Aquinas,[5a] I affirm that Mary's heart is the vital center of her person, the very essence of the personality of the Mother of God.[5b]

The expression "heart of Mary" also refers to all of Mary's free acts and to the history of her earthly existence.

---

4. The meaning of this expression will be clarified in footnote 5 below.
5a. St. Thomas Aquinas, *Summa Theologiae,* Ia, 75.1.
5b. St. John Eudes, in his *Admirable Heart of the Mother of God* has distinguished (Bk. I, chap. 2) the different meanings of the word "heart" in Scripture.

3

Its essential meaning cannot be separated from its "existential" import.[6] Still, there is a uniqueness here. What other human love — totally and exclusively human — was and is, at one and the same time, immaculate and redeemed, virginal and nuptial?

6. For the sense in which I use this word, see my article on "The Existential Mariology of St. Robert Bellarmine," *Marianum,* 1964, pp. 344-6.

The Immaculate Heart of Mary

The grace of the Immaculate Conception signifies "the fullness of redemption in the one who was to welcome the Redeemer,"[7] or in other words the initial plenitude of a created love, infused and habitual (not necessarily actual), in the one who was destined to welcome Uncreated Love. From the first instant of her earthly existence Mary's heart, preserved from all seeds of diabolic hatred or rebellion, was possessed by the infused gift of supernatural love. This gave her complete control over her imagination and sensibility. Thus her first free act, a decisive choice regarding her ultimate end,[8] was an act of pure love and of perfect openness to the grace within her. The three divine Persons dwelt in this pure created love through sanctifying grace, a grace possessed to such a degree that Pope Pius XII, considering the dynamism of the first grace received by Mary, could rightly say:

"The holiness of the Son exceeded and surpassed the holiness of the mother beyond what we can think; but the

---

7. Formula of E. Ortigues.
8. See St. Thomas Aquinas, *Summa Theologiae,* Ia IIa 89.6, a text on which J. Maritain comments in a very interesting way in his *Leçons de philosophie morale,* Paris, Téqui.

vastness of Mary's holiness so far surpasses all other created holiness that she is hidden from the bedazzled gaze of saints and angels in inaccessible heights of splendor."[9]

Was Mary's heart conceived immaculate by Joachim and Anne precisely in order that the Church, a church of angels and men, might be immaculate in love?[10] This conclusion seems to follow from the papal teaching of St. Pius X:

"If Mary was spared from original sin, it is because she was to be the Mother of Christ. But she was the Mother of Christ in order that we might regain hope of eternal life."[11]

To put it in another way: in order that the heavenly Church might be definitively and perfectly immaculate in love, Mary, its principal member, its heart and its mother, was initially conceived immaculate and filled with fair charity, free of all self-love. The text of Pius X states, with all the clarity we could wish for, that the privilege of the Immaculate Conception is ordered to Mary's privileged mission in the economy of redemption; and indeed this could be said of all her other privileges. From its first pulsation the Immaculate Heart is, in the divine plan, the heart of the Church. Mary is Mother of God and she is immaculate so that she can be Mother of the Church.

From this it follows that when the Church honors the heart of her mother with the cult of hyperdulia she is venerating that infused and habitual love of Mary's, perhaps still unconscious but very real, which she gave to the Church from the very first instant of her life. No less is she

---

9. See the original English text in AAS, 46 (1954), 500.

10. See Eph. 1:4.

11. "Eo sane vel magis quia Virgo ipsa expers primaevae labis fuit quod Christi mater futura erat; Christi autem mater fuit, ut nobis aeternorum bonorum spes redintegraretur": encyclical *Ad Diem Illum,* Acts of St. Pius X, Bonne Presse, Paris, Vol. I, p. 86.

honoring that heart's first act of conscious freedom in relation to God, her Creator, and to the entire People of God. This first act of freedom was — a privilege of Mary — an act of pure love which embraced with a single loving regard Uncreated Love and all the creatures willed by Him. It was an act of unconditional surrender to the designs of God. The Church, in honoring this act inspired and sustained by divine grace, wholly informed by the infused and created charity which the Holy Spirit kindles in hearts, honors the act which signalled the Church's distant, future created origin and which is, at the same time, the perfect model of her own offering to Jesus Christ.

It is not merely the present actual love of the risen heart of the Virgin, assumed into glory with her Son, which the Church honors; it is all the love which has gone before, from the first instant of its springing forth. She is honoring the love which already beheld this Church; a love completely human, a love purely spiritual on the one hand — sensible and corporeal on the other. This is the purest love (of a human person) that ever sprang from an immortal soul, yet it is united to a mortal body. It is a love redeemed, radically preserved from all egoism and every possibility of turning into hatred, because of the triple love of its Creator and Redeemer, Jesus — a divine, spiritual and sensible love.

Not only is Mary's heart oriented toward the heart of Jesus, even in advance, but already her ardent charity, *a fountain of living water springing up into eternal life* (John 4:14), is an anticipated effect of the passion and death of the heart of Jesus. The Church's devotion to the heart of his mother has as its final object the heart of Christ, the one who forechose her.

In Mary's predestined love the Church finds the most eloquent personal sign of the love of the Word who pre-arranged all the events of her life. We can say with St. John Damascene:

"Foreknowing your dignity, the God of the universe has loved you; because He loved you, He predestined you, and in the last ages He has called you into existence and made you a mother, that you might bear a God and nourish his own Son and his Word . . . Divine and living masterpiece over whom God the Creator has rejoiced, whose spirit is ruled by God and attentive to God alone, whose whole desire leaps up to Him Who alone is desirable and loveable, whose wrath is directed solely to sin and to the one who engendered it! Your life is loftier than nature; you do not live for your own sake, since it was not for your own sake that you were born. You live to God: for his sake you came into the world, for his sake you will be the handmaid of our salvation, so that God's eternal plan — the Incarnation of the Word and our divinization — may be accomplished through you. *Heart pure and sinless, flawless heart which sees and desires God!*"[12]

We cannot overemphasize the depth of the Damascene formula. In the flowering of her holiness, Mary's heart reflects the immaculate God whom she beholds: *"Blessed are the pure of heart, for they shall see God."* Linked with this purity of Mary's heart is an anger against sin and against the devil who engendered it, wholly informed by divine charity. When the Church venerates the Immaculate Heart of Mary, she also reveres and imitates her loving hatred of sin.

---

12. St. John Damascene, "Homily on the Nativity," Nos. 7, 9 (Sources Chretiennes, No. 80, Cerf, Paris, 1961, pp. 65 and 69-71). I quote the Greek words of the phrase about the heart of Mary: "Kardia katara kai amoluntos, orosa kai potousa theon ton amolunton." I cannot praise too highly the remarkable edition of *Homilies on the Nativity and the Dormition* for which we are indebted to Fr. Pierre Voulet.

The Virginal Heart of Mary

Mary's heart could have been immaculate without being virginal. Precisely because Mary was preserved from actual sin she could, without the least hindrance to her sanctity, have known the pleasures of the flesh. The doctrine of Mary's virginity can in no way be identified with scorn for the role of the flesh in marriage; it is only fully comprehensible and intelligible, in its meaning and finality, because of the One who foresaw its necessity (not intrinsic but "practical"). The actual plan chosen by Divine Providence for the salvation of the world — an economy of redemption through death on the cross — called for virginity on Mary's part.

Insights of speculative theology and of exegesis mutually support each other here. On the one hand, Fr. Guy de Broglie speaks very clearly:

"Mary prepared herself to become the mother of the Savior by her deliberate choice of voluntary virginity, a state of life which from the point of view of womanly nature was equivalent to a choice of renunciation and death. For is it not in a very true sense a deliberate option for death, if a person voluntarily chooses to sterilize in herself all given human powers and desires to perpetuate in offspring the life entrusted to her?

"The significance and finality of this double voluntary

virginity (of Christ and his mother) seems to us all the more indisputable since such a renunciation could in no wise be ascribed, in the case either of Jesus or his *holy mother,* to that humble and cautious mistrust of self which assails other human beings confronted with their own spiritual weakness. On the contrary, escaping the inheritance of Adam's sin, both Jesus and Mary saw in themselves all the goodness of original innocence. Such a renunciation, therefore, could have in them no other motive than expiation for the faults of other human beings, or the light and encouragement that other human beings might draw from their example."[13]

The most recent exegete of "virginity in the Bible," L. Legrand, is, with his methods of literary analysis, in agreement with the orientations of Father de Broglie. He thus concludes his study of "the Lucan spirituality of the daily cross":

"Celibacy is one of the most crucifying forms of this renunciation, one of the most radical ways of taking upon oneself the *nekrosis,* the death of Jesus....In embracing celibacy, one goes so far as to renounce what is perhaps the deepest of human desires — to have children and so to cheat death in a certain sense by seeing one's life prolonged in one's offspring. There is nothing sinful in such a desire. But it constitutes yet another form of trust in the flesh. The disciple who has understood the teaching about the cross has no other hope than that which shines from beyond the cross. He takes up the cross, seen here as the cross of celibacy. Virginity becomes for him a radical way of pushing mortification to the limit, a way demanded by his communion with the crucified Master."

Legrand concludes: "Luke's views on virginity represent

---

13. G. de Broglie, S.J.: *Le principe fondamental de la theologie mariale,* in *Maria,* Vol. VI, pp. 342-3 and 328 (see pp. 343-6), Beauchesne, Paris, 1961.

a theological advance. The Christian celibate points to the cross."[14]

Then our author applies this interpretation to the Lucan presentation of the mystery of Mary:

"If it is true that the Infancy Gospel is thus supported by a paschal typology, and if, for Luke, virginity is an anticipated participation in the Passion, while the intervention of the Spirit in the conception of Jesus anticipates the Resurrection, it becomes highly probable that Luke saw, beyond the mystery of Mary's virginal fruitfulness, the outline of the cross. Mary's fruitful virginity foreshadows the life-giving death of Jesus. The Virgin, like the cross, represents the weakness of the flesh transformed into power through the action of the Spirit of life. In the theology of the Infancy Gospel, Mary's virginity signifies poverty and weakness; it plays the role of the cross in Pauline theology. The *tapeinosis* (not humility, but humiliation, like the Hebrew *oni* or distress, misery) of the Virgin takes all its meaning from its similarity to the *etapeinosen* of Calvary (Phil. 2:8)."[15]

This, for Luke, is the meaning of Mary's virginity. And for Mary herself? Although Legrand does not wish to take a stand on this point,[16] I believe it perfectly possible, in light of the information he has supplied, to hold that the immaculate young Israelite, familiar with the Scriptures, and no less with the Servant songs than with Anna's canticle, freely opted for virginity in a sacrificial context, confronted as she was with the world's sin and the pride often accom-

14. L. Legrand, *La virginite dans la bible,* Cerf, Paris, 1964, 59-61.
15. Ibid., pp. 116, 117, 118. Compare with Phil. 2:8 and Lk. 1:52 (exaltation).
16. Ibid., p. 15.

panying physical generation.[17] It was in a fully deliberate manner that the "handmaid of the Lord" chose a humiliating virginity, a point Legrand does not sufficiently stress at the close of his exegetical analysis when he rightly affirms:

"Mary can be compared with Anna. Her 'humiliation' as a virgin is analogous to Anna's sterility. As an authentic Jewish girl, she does not consider her virginity a title to glory but rather a kind of annihilation, a form of impoverishment, a state of humiliation. Mary expresses this in the Magnificat. Being a virgin, she was lowly, but her opprobrium was taken away. She was scorned, but now she is proclaimed blessed (Luke 1:48). Poor, she has been exalted (Luke 1:52); empty, she has been filled (Luke 1:53) . . . In the perspective of Luke's first two chapters, Mary's virginity is therefore a total poverty, a privation not only of the goods of this world but even of that which gave women, in Israel, the right to respect."[18]

The very humble heart of the Immaculate One saw this humiliating condition of virginity, without "title to glory" before men, a real strength (which Legrand does not seem to treat adequately),[19] a gift of God which permitted her to glorify her Creator, offended by the sensual pride of so many.

---

17. We know that St. John of the Cross denounced the pride that might insinuate itself even into the desire to have many children . . . the danger today seems less, but can it not still be found in a rural civilization?
18. Legrand, op. cit., pp. 117-118.
19. Legrand, crit, p. 117: "Mary compares herself to Anna. Her 'humiliation' as a virgin is analogous to that of the sterile Anna. In Anna's case her misery consists in being childless." But further on (p. 143), Legrand clarifies: "Like Christ's death, Mary's virginity has not merely a negative value. It is not just a privation: she is already rich in all the detachment and abandonment to God's will which sums up man's attitude, conscious as he is of his weakness in this world marked by death."

This is the explanation, as Donnelly[20] and Holzmeister[21] rightly remark in agreement with St. Bernard and in disagreement with certain Fathers, of the question Mary put to the angel: *How can this be, since I have no husband?* (Luke 1:34). She signifies at one and the same time her resolution to maintain her virginity, as certain Protestant exegetes themselves recognize,[22] and her availability to a divine plan differing from her own, which may require that she "should know man." It is for this reason, and this is a point which Legrange makes with precision as well as subtlety, that Mary speaks in the present rather than the future tense.[23] Mary was disposed to submit completely to God's will, even by accepting marriage; she only wanted to be sure that the eventual renunciation of her initial resolve, which she had formed under the inspiration of grace, would be in conformity with his will.

Clearly, then, Mary's virginity, physical and perpetual, was primarily a free decision of her immaculate heart influenced by the Spirit, a co-redemptive renunciation of the worldly glory of physical motherhood, a renunciation oriented to reparation for the sake of the People of God. It was an act of love, not only for God, but also for proud and sensual mankind.

Reciprocally, and as an indirect consequence, Mary's choice of virginity was to color and enhance with a special beauty not only the love she bore her Creator, but also her love for all men. Mary loves each person with a virginal love, wholly focused on the God within.

---

20. See Carol, *Mariologia,* BAC, Madrid, 1964, p. 631.
21. U. Holzmeister, *Virum non cognosco, Verbum Domini,* 19 (1939), p. 74.
22. Donnelly quotes Klostermann, Kattenbusch, Rengstorf (Carol, *Mariologia,* 627).
23. Lagrange, *Luke,* Gabalda, Paris, 1927, p. 33.

This virginal love for mankind in God, and the free and willing decision which gave rise to it, are honored by the Church when she practices devotion to the heart of Mary, her own virginal heart. What St. Augustine said about the Church is most perfectly realized in the heart of Mary:

"The whole Church is called a virgin . . . all (the members) preserve virginity of mind. What is virginity of mind? Entire faith, firm hope, sincere charity."[24]

From this viewpoint Mary's physical virginity appears as a sacramental sign of the immaculate integrity of her heart and the virginal integrity of the Church.

---

24. St. Augustine, *In Jo.,* 13.12 ML, 35, 1499.

The Nuptial Heart of Mary

In the context of a Jewish society where consecrated celibacy was practiced only by marginal groups of Essenes, one might think that, *subjectively,* the Virgin Mary chose[25] as her husband Joseph, the just man predestined[26] for this mission, precisely to better guard the virginity she had vowed. But *objectively* this virginal marriage had still other purposes in the divine plan, as St. Robert Bellarmine teaches:[27] to preserve the Virgin from the suspicion of

---

25. "Ipsa elegit conjugium," writes St. Robert Bellarmine, loc. cit. See Donnelly, loc. cit., pp. 626-7. I note that Luther and Calvin also taught Mary's virginity after childbirth, as Max Thurian stresses in *Mary, the Mother of all Christians,* Herder and Herder, N.Y. 1964, p. 39.

26. The expression is that of St. Irenaeus (*Adversus Haereses,* III, 32.4; P.G. 7.959 A).

27. This accords with a long patristic tradition. See my article cited above, p. 350. We have to recognize that classical authors limited themselves to this analysis of objective motives for a virginal marriage, without going into these subjective motives. We can better understand the psychology of Mary and Joseph with the help of an example borrowed from the history of the Christian missions in Korea at the beginning of the 19th century. When Christianity was introduced there by persons coming from China, a young man and woman of the new Church in Korea, wishing to preserve their virginity, could find no other way of doing this by contracting marriage for this purpose!

adultery and to help her in the rearing of the Child-God.

In this virginal marriage a growing and ever more unique love for St. Joseph filled Mary's heart. Himself a virgin through her[28] and for her, he was the guardian of her virginity; together with her he was to rear the Man-God, Messiah and Savior. The name of Jesus, conferred jointly[29] by Mary and Joseph in obedience to the divine will upon the Son of God, of Adam and of David, was the supreme bond of this indissolubly virginal and nuptial love.

In heaven as on earth, Mary's heart loves Joseph with this unique love which she has not, nor could have, for any other creature. Who else could have the right to so intimate a love? St. Joseph is the exceptional friend, the unique friend of Mary, better loved by her than the most perfect of angels or saints, and the one whom she would wish to be holier than any other creature. Mary knew she owed to Joseph her honor, her life — were it not for him, says St. Jerome, she could have been stoned —, her daily bread; she knew she owed to him, together with the preservation of her own virginity, Jesus Himself, who could only have been virginally conceived within her, thanks to the virginity of St. Joseph.[30]

In honoring Mary's heart it would be impossible to exclude St. Joseph, the privileged object of her love. Save for a few exceptions, and some partial and local treatments, this love and this marriage have not yet found, in Marian

---

28. See the celebrated text of St. Jerome: "Vindico ipsum Joseph virginem fuisse per Mariam ut ex virginali coniugio virgo filius nasceretur," *Advs. Helv.* 19, ML 23.213.

29. Joseph and Mary each independently received from God the mission of giving Jesus his name, with all that that implied in the Semitic world: Mt. 1:21; Lk. 1:31.

30. See Sauve, *Saint Joseph intime,* Gigord, Paris, 1928, pp. 208-9 and 255-6.

syntheses, the place they deserve.[31] Could the reason perhaps be that their ecclesial significance has not been sufficiently noted, as Sauve perceives?[32]

"God," he tells us, "had decided from all eternity to give his Son to the world, but to give Him only through this virginal marriage. This marriage was all the more true in that it was the sign and the most perfect proof, after the Incarnation, of the union of Jesus with his Church. This union, which the marriage of Joseph and Mary heralded, He inaugurated in all perfection. Thus the union of Jesus with his Church could be but the prolongation, necessarily less perfect, of the marriage vivified by the presence of Jesus. For with what souls would Jesus be as intimately, as deeply united in the future as with Mary and Joseph, since it was in Him and through Him that they were united to each other?"[33]

The Church is the virginal Spouse of Christ her Savior; her nuptials are sacramentally represented and rendered present by all Christian marriages. Therefore the Church, in her love for Mary's irrevocable choice of a virginal marriage, and her heart's unique nuptial love for St. Joseph, is loving the very conditions and sources of her own existence.

The Church also cherishes the faithful and indissoluble love for St. Joseph which she perceives in Mary's immaculate heart because it is a model for her, and a meritorious cause of her own invincible love for Jesus. It is a chaste love and a source of conjugal chastity for Christian spouses. Contemplating it, they receive the strength to follow more easily the Apostle Paul's suggestion: "Do not refuse one

31. In the great syntheses of Mariology (notably *Maria*) the marriage of Mary and Joseph is mentioned, but rather, it seems, in connection with other things than as the object of a special study in a separate chapter.
32. Sauve, op. cit., pp. 71 ff.
33. Sauve, op. cit., 74-5.

17

another except perhaps by agreement for a season, so as to give yourselves to prayer'' (I Cor. 7:5).

The Church knows, furthermore, that it is by imaging this virginal marriage, her prototype, that she has been led to discover more clearly that "the essence of marriage consists in the indivisible union of spirits, in virtue of which the spouses are obliged to preserve mutual fidelity," as St. Thomas Aquinas noted.[34] Contemplation of the virginal marriage of Mary and Joseph has led the Church to realize that a marriage is already true before being physically consummated.

Prayerful consideration of this unique marriage may have been a partial occasion of the audacious contract whereby St. John Eudes took Mary for his mystical spouse.[35]

It is clear therefore, that the Church's cult of the heart of Mary glorifies the virginal and nuptial heart of Joseph's spouse. In this light Mary is seen as the heart of a Church which is both virgin and spouse.

34. St. Thomas Aquinas, *Summa Theologiae,* III, 29, 2.
35. See the saint's contract of alliance with the Mother of God which he signed in his blood at the age of 66 in 1668; Emile Georges, *St. John Eudes,* Lethielleux, Paris, 1925, pp. 492-7.

The Heart of Mary,
Mother of the Redeeming God

For the Church, Mary's heart is above all the heart of the mother of her Savior. In dependence upon the Holy Spirit it is the origin and life principle of the heart of Jesus.

Some theologians, who are also mystics, rival each other in affirming this. Thus, St. Francis Borgia: "Mary conceived the Son of God in her spirit through faith, in her heart through love, and in her flesh and her womb by clothing Him with this flesh for our redemption."[36] Retaining more clearly the physical and corporeal sense of the word "heart," and not merely its symbolic meaning, St. John Eudes was to write a century later: ". . . This heart, which is not only the life principle of the Child Jesus, but also the origin of the virginal blood with which his sacred humanity was formed in the womb of his mother . . . this heart, the most notable and venerable part of that virginal body which gave a body to the eternal Word; this heart, the life principle of our Head, is consequently the life principle of his members."[37]

---

36. St. Francis Borgia, *Tratados espirituales,* ed. Dalmases, Juan Flors, Barcelona, 1964, p. 52.

These very clear statements make explicit what had long lain implicit in the Church's thought regarding the divine maternity. Although St. Augustine had already stated with precision that there was an inseparable physical and moral[38] bond between Mary and Jesus, the declarations of the Council of Ephesus seemed to retain only the physical aspect of the mystery: Mary is the Mother of God because she "engendered, according to the flesh, the Word of God made flesh."[39] It is true that the West was not fully represented, numerically speaking, at this Council. The decisive importance of Vatican Council II, from this point of view, was surely that it integrated in the *Dogmatic Constitution on the Church* what modern theologians, inspired by Scheeben, have called "the integral concept of the divine maternity," perceived as a real ontological relationship of physical motherhood, but also as a moral

---

37. St. John Eudes, *Coeur admirable de la Mere de Dieu,* Book XI, meditation for the sixth day of the octave of the feast of the Heart of Mary, second point. *Oeuvres choisies,* Lethellieux, Paris, 1932, Vol. II, p. 350.

38. I quote these texts from St. Augustine: "Illa virgo Christum . . . spiritualiter credendo concepit" (*in Ps.* 67, 21; ML, 36, 826); "fides in mente, Christus in ventre" (*sermo* 166,1; ML,38, 1010). It is true that Augustine said elsewhere (*de Virginitate,* Ch. 6): "mater quidem spiritu, *non* capitis nostri." There is no real contradiction here: in the same sentence, Augustine writes: "ex quo [Christo] *magis* illa [Maria] spiritualiter nata." The *magis* tempers the weight of the *non*. On the speculative plane the agreement would be posited thus: "the holy and free acceptance of her motherhood [by Mary] is an anticipation of the merits acquired by the action of the Man-God. Thus the man Jesus intervenes at the heart of her concrete maternity, to which God has called her. The merits of Mary flow entirely from Christ's merits" (E. Schillebeeckx, O.P., *Marie, Mere de la Redemption,* Cerf, Paris, 1963, p. 90).

39. See Dz. S. 252.

relationship of love and devotion, terminating as well in the Word.[40] This seems to follow from one clear text chosen from among others: "Mary, who at the message of the angel received the Word of God *in her heart and body . . .*"[41] Ephesus was content to anathematize those who denied the divine motherhood, affirming it according to the flesh without deeping its nature and implications, and to proclaim the role of Mary's freedom in the realization of the mystery of the Incarnation. In God's designs it was left to Vatican Council II to give us a more complete view of the divine motherhood, a view more balanced and in harmony with our modern concern for subjectivity and freedom. Incontestably, this is doctrinal progress; it has not been widely commented upon elsewhere. It may partially explain Protestant heresy, so negative in regard to Mary's entire active role in the mystery of the Incarnation.[42] Between Ephesus and Vatican II we have Luther, Calvin and Barth.[43]

If the Protestant world of today were to return to St. Augustine, whose disciples Luther and Calvin claimed to be, they would discover with the Doctor of Grace that "Mary conceived the flesh of Christ by faith,"[44] and that

<hr>

40. See M.J. Nicolas: "Le concept integral de Maternite divine," *Revue Thomiste,* 1937; *Theotokos,* Descle, 1965, pp. 72-5.
41. Dogmatic Constitution *Lumen Gentium,* No. 53.
42. See *Lumen Gentium* No. 56: "The holy Fathers see [Mary] as used by God not merely in a passive way, but as cooperating in the work of human salvation through free faith and obedience." When composing this sentence, were they perhaps thinking of Barth?
43. See my analysis of the Barthian position, and the Catholic use I make of certain aspects, in my article on the Mariology of St. Robert Bellarmine, "Marianum," 1964, pp. 344-5 and 381-6.
44. St. Augustine, ML, 42, 490. I again quote these other texts of St. Augustine: "Non concupiscentia carnis urente, sed fidei caritate dervente" (Sermo 214, 6); "non enim eum Virgo libidine, sed fide concepit" (Sermo 69, 3, 4).

in consequence, the heart of Mary played a decisive role in the salvation of mankind. Fr. René Laurentin speaks emphatically in this regard: "Mary's divine motherhood is prepared by her faith, proposed to her faith, accomplished by virtue of a consent which is an act of faith. This act of perfect faith, achieved through love, is meritorious."[45]

Although the Christian East — I am thinking, for example, of St. John Damascene[46] — did not completely ignore the role of Mary's loving freedom and faith at the time of the Incarnation, it must be admitted that Western theology, developing the thought of St. Augustine, has deepened it remarkably. Surely St. Robert Bellarmine reached a summit in his interpretation of Mary's response to the angel Gabriel: *"Behold, I am the handmaid of the Lord, let it be done to me according to your word."* The Jesuit Doctor perceives, as we have explained at length elsewhere,[47] an obedient consent to grace, an option and a free decision, a desire and a prayer: " 'I choose and ask that it be done to me according to your word.' She herself chose to be made the Mother of God."

Going still further, it would be true to say that it is due to this response, made at this precise instant, that the heart of Mary became the heart of the Mother of God and of the Church, the heart of the very Church which she now bore within her. Carrying Jesus in her womb, Mary also carried all those whose life would be contained within the life of the Savior. All of us who are united to Christ should own

---

45. R. Laurentin, *Court traité de Théologie Mariale,* Lethielleux, Paris, 1959, p. 98.
46. St. John Damascene, *Homélie sur la Dormition,* I, 7 to the end; Voulet, p. 101. I shall use the following initials in quoting from Damascene: D. I, D. II, D. III to designate each of his homilies on the Dormition, indicating immediately after the letter V, the page number in the edition of P. Voulet (Sources Chrétiennes, No. 80).
47. B. de Margerie, article cited, 355-61; see in particular note 27a.

that we have been born from Mary's womb," wrote St. Pius X.[48] In a more rigorous style, Vatican Council II opened up new co-redemptive perspectives on the *Ecce ancilla Domini*: "By thus consenting to the divine utterance, Mary, a daughter of Adam, became the mother of Jesus. Embracing God's saving will with a full heart (*pleno corde*) and impeded by no sin, she devoted herself totally as a handmaid of the Lord to the person and work of her Son. In subordination to him and along with him, by the grace of almighty God she served the mystery of redemption."[49]

The work of the Son is, obviously, the Church. Mary is handmaid and mother, *doule kai meter* as St. John Damascene put it so well, not only of Christ but also of the Church.[50] As the Church proclaimed Mary her mother through the voice of Pope Paul VI, so, too, she proclaims in the text of *Lumen Gentium,* now under discussion, that the Queen of the world has made herself a handmaid for the triumph of the redemptive work of Jesus. There is no contradiction here: is not motherhood service, even slavery for love? A mother willingly puts herself at the service of her children, becomes a slave for the sake of their health. Handmaid of the Redeemer, Mary necessarily places herself at the service of her children who have been redeemed by Him. She is the slave of love.[51]

Vatican Council II thus establishes a close connection between the divine motherhood and Christ's redemptive work. The texts already cited, like those which we shall give below,

---

48. St. Pius X, *Ad diem illum,* op. cit., pp. 76-7. See St. Leo the Great: "Generatio Christi origo est populi christiani," ML, 54, 213, B.
49. Dogmatic Constitution *Lumen Gentium,* No. 56. We will use the reference: LG.
50. St. John Damascene, D. III, 5 (V.195). The two words are evangelical.
51. If the Mother of God made herself, and was, the slave of love of the Church and of humanity, would this not make St. Louis Grignon de Montfort's spiritual doctrine more logical and understandable?

encourage us to agree with Father de Broglie as to the first principle of Catholic Mariology: "Mary, far from being simply the Mother of God, is essentially the mother of a redeeming God, who came among us to associate us all (beginning with his mother herself) with his own salvific sacrifice."[52] I think that this formula sums up, better than any other, the fundamental aim of Chapter 8 of *Lumen Gentium.* Mary is not only Christ's mother according to the flesh, she is also his mother in his role of Redeemer.

Although it may seem at first glance that Vatican Council II makes no mention of the heart of Mary, our textual examination has already shown us that this omission is only apparent. In reality the conciliar constitution explaizes the fact that it is Mary's heart (heart in every sense of the word) which welcomes the redeeming Word and gives Him to the world: "Mary, the Mother of God and Mother of the Redeemer, received the Word of God in her heart and in her body and gave Life to the world."[53] *Lumen Gentium* explicitly states that it is an act of Mary's heart perceived as immaculate: "with a full heart and impeded by no sin."[54]

Precisely because Mary freely accepts to be the Mother of God our Savior, in an act of pure love for God and humanity which ratifies and prolongs her first free act, her virginal heart becomes, at the time of the Incarnation, the heart of the redeemed Church (cf. Eph. 5:23). The Church is thus *conceived* in and by this virginal heart under the action of the Holy Spirit, the invisible Spouse of Mary. The heart of Mary is, from the moment of her acceptance and consent to the message of the Annunciation, the immaculate heart of an immaculate Church, — albeit made up of stained

---

52. G. de Broglie, S.J., op. cit., *Maria,* VI, p. 331.
53. LG, 53.
54. LG, 56.

members.[55] Hers is the heart of the mother, queen and handmaid of the Church. This has been providentially ordained so that the Church, already conceived in Mary's heart, may be born of her and of her tears at the same time that it is born of the wounded heart of the Redeemer as He hangs upon the cross — He, the Redeemer of both Mary and the Church.

Scheeben expressed the redemptive and ecclesial mystery of the Annunciation with incomparable depth when he wrote: "Mary's role finds a perfect analogy in the human heart. The head is nourished by the heart's blood, and owes its material existence to it. Reciprocally, the head communicates life to the heart through the nerves, thus enabling it to do its proper work."[56] Christ, as Mary's Creator God and her Head, still owes his human existence to her, and gives to her, more fully than to any other created person, the abundant outpouring of his Spirit, the soul of the Church. The Word of divine Goodness assumes a human heart thanks to the generosity He has Himself placed in the loving heart of Mary.[57] In the Mystical Body of Jesus, Mary, mother of the Head, is the heart.

---

55. See St. Ambrose: "ex maculatis immaculate," in Lk. 1:17 (ML, 15, 1540-4).
56. Scheeben, op. cit., pp. 71-2.
57. St. Thomas Aquinas speaks several times of the *Verbum bonitatis* (*divinae*): *Summa Theologiae* I, 30, 1, 2; I, 30, 2, 4; especially I, 27, 5, 2.

The Compassionate and Co-redemptive Heart of Mary Who Has Been Redeemed

"The heart of the Virgin," wrote St. Lawrence Justinian, "was created to be a very clear mirror reflecting the passion of Christ and a perfect image of his death."[58] Let us say further: Mary's heart shared in a unique way in the sacrifice of our Redeemer. We could summarize and synthesize the teaching of Vatican Council II on this subject in the following affirmation: Mary was redeemed in advance in order that she might be our unique co-redemptrix under, and with, her and our sole Redeemer, Jesus. *Lumen Gentium* explicitly affirms that Mary's role in our redemption had been merited by Christ; that it was privileged, even unique; physical and spiritual, sorrowful and maternal.[59] It delineates the essence and intimate nature of her maternal cooperation as a sorrowing, loving consent to Jesus' death, a consent which ratified and prolonged the consent she had made at the time of the

---

58. "Factum est Cor Cirginis speculum clarissimum passionis Christi, et imago perfecta mortis eius": St. Lawrence Justinian, *De Triumphali Christi Agone,* Ch. XXI.
59. See the justification for these affirmations in LG, 60, 61, 58, 61-2.

Annunciation. Her participation included the simultaneous exercise of the moral virtue of obedience and of the three theological virtues. In brief, it shows us Mary's part in the work of redemption, springing from her heart.

This seems to be an accurate interpretation of the following conciliar text: ". . . suffering grievously with her only-begotten Son, she united herself *with a maternal heart* to his sacrifice, and *lovingly* consented to the immolation of this Victim which she herself had brought forth."[60] Above all it throws light upon this most important doctrinal paragraph: ". . . united with [her Son] in suffering as he died on the cross, *in an utterly singular way she cooperated,* by her obedience, faith, hope and burning charity, in the Savior's work of restoring supernatural life to souls. For this reason she is a mother to us in the order of grace."[61]

The doctrinal affirmation of the 1964 Council regarding Mary's singular cooperation in the work of the Redeemer brings to mind, almost irresistibly, the dogmatic definition of 1854 concerning the lofty mode of Mary's own redemption: "Redeemed in the most sublime manner . . . she cooperated in a unique way in the work of the Savior."

Blessed Duns Scotus demonstrated that the Immaculate Conception and the universal redemptive mission of Jesus were not opposed, and that Jesus redeemed the Immaculate One. In a parallel movement, Vatican Council II suggests that the redemption (passive) of Mary by Jesus and her privileged and unique cooperation in the active redemption of all the other offspring of Adam, not only are not opposed, but are firmly united by the bond of final causality. This is clear in the conciliar text already quoted: "Impeded by no sin, she gave herself totally as a handmaid of the Lord. In subordination to him and along with him she served the

---

60. LG, 58.
61. LG, 61.

mystery of redemption."[62] How can we fail to conclude from these texts that Mary was redeemed by the crucified Christ in a unique and exceptional manner precisely in order that she could be the sole sub-redemptrix," the one "Co-redemptrix" of the Church and of humanity, in dependence upon their and her unique Redeemer? How can we fail to conclude that she was redeemed by her Son and Lord to the point of receiving the grace of being Co-redemptrix?

The suffering heart of Mary, pierced with a sword[63] of sorrow by men who loved darkness better than light, (cf. Lk. 2:35 and Jn. 3:19) thus played a decisive role in their passage from the darkness of hatred to the light of love, from death to life (cf. I Jn. 2:9 and 3:14). Scheeben had already expressed in biblical and patristic imagery what Vatican Council II was to teach in more abstract terms:

"In the image-language of Scripture and the Fathers the redemption of the world was effected through the blood of the Lamb, the ransom, and through the sigh of the Dove, prayer sanctified by the Holy Spirit and offered in the name of the redeemed that the ransom might be accepted. Or again, this redemption was realized by the act of the Head and his priestly power, and on the other hand by the love of the heart and the groans of the spouse. This heart was itself a perpetual sacrifice through its loving participation in the sufferings of the Lamb....Mary's collaboration in the sacrifice of Christ receives its perfect expression when we consider her heart as a living altar erected for humanity. Upon this altar the oblation sprung from her womb is offered by Christ....In this manner Christ the Victim is

_____

62. LG, 56; See Carol, *Mariologia* (BAC), Madrid, 1964, pp. 797-8.
63. See P. Benoit, O.P.: "Un glaive transpercera l'ame," *Catholic Bible Quarterly,* Vol. XXV, 1963, pp. 251-61.

not only taken *from* humanity and offered *by* it, but is offered *within* it.

"Mary, 'Theotokos,' is also 'the one who offers the Victim': an after-type of the Ark of the Covenant when she carries Christ *beneath* her heart and nourishes him with her blood, an after-type of the throne of propitiation when she carries him *in* her heart while he sheds his blood and sprinkles her with it."[64]

Jesus dies with the full and loving consent of his mother; but this new and supreme consent, ultimate ratification of the *Ecce ancilla Domini* of the *Fiat* of the Annunciation,[65] is merited and wrought by his very death itself.[66] Jesus Christ offers Himself to the Father for all his brethren on the altar of the immaculate and broken heart of Mary, through the holocaust of her maternal freedom. The visible sacrifice of Jesus is the sacrament, or sacred and efficacious sign, of the invisible sacrifice of Mary and of humanity.

We may say to the compassionate heart of Mary standing at the foot of the cross (Jn. 19:25) what St. John Damascene said to the Virgin of the Annunciation: "Be joyful! You are the ewe giving birth to the Lamb of God, you are the instrument of our salvation."[67]

In the grievously loving exercise of her activity as Co-redemptrix, Mary places all the powers granted to her divine motherhood, state and dignity entirely at the Redeemer's disposal for the triumph of his redemptive work. By her faith in his saving Blood, and in his Divinity and future Resurrection, she enters freely into the sacrifice of her agonizing Son, assenting to the immolation of the body

---

64. Scheeben, op. cit., pp. 181-2 and 185-6.
65. LG, 62.
66. LG, 60.
67. St. John Damascene, Ch. III, 5 (V, 195).

she had engendered according to the flesh. Hence, she merits to bring to spiritual birth, in tears, grief and love, the members of the only Son of her virginal heart. With the hour of Jesus, Mary's hour has come (cf. Jn. 16:21 and 2:4). Her heart, which had conceived the universal Church at the time of the Annunciation, now brings it to birth and gives it to the world. Jesus crucified proclaims her Mother of the Church, symbolized by John:[68] *Behold your Mother*! (Jn. 19:27). His proclamation declares, rather than establishes, a fact. In the same way Pope Paul VI's proclamation in 1964 simply made this same fact manifest. In consenting anew, Mary freely accepts to be the servant of this universal Church which she had conceived in joyous faith, before having brought it to birth in tears. The new Eve is united with the new Adam.

But Mary at the foot of the cross is not merely the Mother of the Church. She is its principal and supereminent member. At this moment Mary's heart is, in a very special way, the heart of the Church. When almost all the other members are unfaithful to the Head, the heart remains more vitally united to Him than ever in the name of the entire Body. If St. John symbolizes the Church — daughter of Mary according to the teaching of St. Laurence Justinian — Mary herself symbolizes the Church[69] seen as a community bonded in charity, a society of love. She is its *transcendent* type. In the Church she is the heart watching in faith while many sleep the sleep of unbelief. She is the heart which causes the blood, that is, charity, to flow throughout the body. Mary's heart, at the foot of the cross, is the loving heart of the loving Church.

Alone, standing at the foot of the cross, Mary preserves

---

68. See St. Lawrence Justinian, *De triumphali Christi Agone,* Ch. 18; see the text in *Marianum,* 26 (1964), 320-1.
69. St. Ambrose in *Lucam,* Bk. VII, 5; ML, 15, 1787.

faith in redemptive Love totally and perfectly.[70] She personifies the Church participating in its own salvation, as she, at the same time, efficiently causes this participation. "God has willed that the redeeming act of Christ the Head, who represents us before the Father, should be accompanied by Mary's act of adherence, in which she represents the Church."[71]

The Church is a hierarchical communion established in faith, hope and love, and these three find their source in the believing and hoping love of Mary, its mother and heart. Mary, "model of the Church in the matter of faith, hope and perfect union with Christ," according to the teaching of Vatican Council II,[72] is not only a type of the Church but its model. She is also its type because, especially on Calvary, she was personally engaged in bringing about in the other members of the ecclesial community what Christ crucified had already typically effected in her through his compassion for her: the triumph of love's sacrifice and oblation.[73]

In the tabernacle of her womb Mary clothed the Word of Life in the priestly garment of his mortal flesh, so that

---

70. See Binder, *Maria et Ecclesia* (Rome, International Marian Academy, 1959), Vol. III, "in passione Domini fidem Ecclesiae in B. Virgine sola remansisse," pp. 389-488 and especially p. 486.

71. C. Dillenschneider, C. Ss. R., *Marie dans la creation renovee,* Alsatia, Paris, 1957, p. 242. The pastor De Saussure (*Contemplation de la Croix,* pp. 73-4) wrote: "God made man, you have loved in her your Church made woman. Image of God invisible, you have restored for us in her the image of the invisible Church: behold your Mother."

72. LG, 63. St. Bernard calls Mary "Mater charitatis" (ML, 183, 933). See on this subject the article of P. Narciso Garcia Garces, C.M.P.: "El Corazon de Maria visto por S. Bernardo," *Estudios Marianos,* XIV, II-36.

73. See the considerations of Schillebeeckx (op. cit. pp. 128-9) on the dynamic and active character of the notion of type as applied to Mary in relation to the Church.

He might officiate as our Sovereign Priest on the altar of the Cross.[74] On Golgotha she becomes — and here we return to Scheeben's thought[75] — the deaconess of Christ's priestly sacrifice. She is both the representative of the People of God and, through her divine motherhood, the consecrated minister of the Sovereign Priest — heart and mother of the Church. "In this way Mary is given a true share in the sacrifice of Christ," a share which in no way denies "the independence and authority of Christ's action," wrote Scheeben (ibid.). The expression "share" calls for immediate qualification.

Without going into a technical study of the doctrine of Marian co-redemption,[76] I may say that the Church, in venerating and loving Mary's wounded and glorified heart, loves and venerates with filial gratitude, her meritorious and atoning love. Mary, as Co-redemptrix, offered to the Father the sacrifice of the one Redeemer for all the children of Adam. The Church venerates this created, redeemed and co-redeeming love of the one who gave her birth and ever maintains her in life. She loves her own heart, that heart which gives her the Blood, price of her redemption and her immortal libation.

No man ever hates his own flesh, but nourishes it and cherishes it (Eph. 5:29). The Church reaches the heights of love proper to her when she loves her own heart, Mary her mother, the maternal heart of the universal Church. How can she ever forget what her mother has suffered in order to give her life (cf. Sirach 7:27)? "Through you, Virgin Mary, we draw from the fountains of salvation, from the wounds of Christ."[77]

---

74. See St. Bonaventure, *Sermon IV de Annuntiatione.*
75. Scheeben, op. cit., pp. 184-5.
76. See on this subject Dillenschneider (op. cit., 161-76) and Carol (*Mariologia,* BAC, 1964, p. 794).
77. Third Nocturn of Matins of the Office of the Seven Dolors of the Virgin Mary, September 15.

The Heart of Mary, Heart of the Church's Eucharistic Life

"All these with one accord devoted themselves to prayer together with . . . Mary, the mother of Jesus," says the author of the Acts of the Apostles, describing the life of the early Church after the Resurrection and Ascension of the Lord and before Pentecost (Acts 1:14). Mary was so filled with faith in the Resurrection of her Son that she alone had no need to go to the tomb or to be reassured by a vision. She became the non-hierarchical spiritual center, the visible affective pole of the ecclesial community. Living in St. John's home, she called nothing her own, but she and her new-born children "had everything in common and distribution was made to each as any had need" (Acts 4:32-5). If "the multitude of believers were of one heart and soul," this was clearly because, even after Pentecost, they "devoted themselves to prayer with Mary" (Acts 4:32; 1:14).

It was the visible presence of Mary praying that gave the primitive Church but one heart and soul — in a very profound sense, the heart and soul of Mary. Bossuet has expressed this idea in magnificent terms:

"She [Mary] saw her Son in all his members. Her compassion was a prayer for all who suffered; her heart was in the heart of all who groaned, to help them to cry for mercy, in the wounds of all the wounded to help them beg for relief, in all loving hearts to urge them to run to console the needy and afflicted, in all the apostles to proclaim the Gospel, in all the martyrs to shed their blood, and finally in all the faithful to observe Christ's precepts, listen to his counsel and follow his example."[78]

Living in John's home, Mary not only retold the good news of the Incarnation, of her own virginal motherhood, of the childhood of the Savior and other happenings in the public life of Jesus and of the whole community of the faithful. She was there preeminently as the Praying One, participating in a unique manner in the Eucharistic sacrifice, just as she had participated in a unique manner in the sacrifice of the cross.

In order to understand fully Mary's role in the mystery of the Eucharist, we need to reread the Johannine account of the wedding feast at Cana and the corresponding scene of Jesus' farewell to his mother, in light of the period of the history of the Church[79] in which they were composed and promulgated. I propose to sketch this briefly here.

Numerous commentators on St. John, Bouyer and Charlier among others, stress the Eucharistic and ecclesial significance of the miracle worked at the marriage feast at Cana. In recounting this miracle, John, in order to render the Eucharistic mystery foreshadowed there more easily credible, wished to make it clear to his readers that the

---

78. Bossuet, *Sermon II sur l'Assomption* (1663) Point 1 (Lebarcq, Vol. IV). This text becomes clearer in the light of note 180: Bossuet does not intend to show a physical presence of Mary's heart in others, but a moral influence.

79. See the Instruction of the Pontifical Biblical Commission of April 21, 1964, on "the historical truth of the Gospels," in particular what is said about the role of the Apostles in the second stage of transmission (Doc. Cath., col. 713-4; see the commentaries of Cardinal Bea, col. 783-6).

intercession of the Mother of Jesus played the role of non-hierarchic mediation in the Eucharistic celebration in which they were taking part. Just as Mary, by her consent to the Incarnation, provided the body for the sacrifice, so also she obtained through her intercession the transformation of the bread and wine into the Body and Blood of Jesus.

In the early days of the Church Mary must have constantly repeated her prayer to the Sovereign Priest in heaven, "They have no [or not enough] wine." Here, she would be referring to the wine of charity with which those who drink the Blood of the Lamb are inebriated. She must, too, have unceasingly urged all Christians, "Do whatever he tells you," and by this she would mean, "Drink the Blood of my Son as he has commanded you." Obedience to the law of love would be sacramentally signified by the Eucharist.

Again, when St. John emphasizes (2:11) that at Cana Jesus "manifested his glory" and that "his disciples believed in him," it is abundantly clear that he is preparing his readers to understand the profound meaning of what he will report in 19:26: "Behold your son! Behold your mother!" It is the mother who transmits life. It was Mary who, through her prayer, obtained that first sign, thanks to which John, surely present at Cana, came to believe that Jesus was sent from the Father and that the believing disciples had thus "passed from death to life." In Johannine language, to believe means to have eternal life: "He who hears my word and believes him who sent me has eternal life" (Jn. 5:24). When, therefore, Jesus said to John "Behold your mother," for John this meant "Behold the one who, by her prayer, has obtained eternal life for you through faith in me." John knew well that "that which is born of flesh [meaning here John's mother Salome, present on Calvary: Mk. 15:40] is flesh and that which is born of the Spirit is spirit" (Jn. 3:6). He understood that at Cana he had been reborn of the Spirit and of Mary.

The new Eve, mother of the living, could say once more,

"They have no wine." Now that Jesus' hour was come, Mary saw the Apostles in flight and noted John's weakening faith in the imminent Resurrection. She could well remember that prayer of hers which had first won them their faith. In spite of this they now remained blind before the supreme manifestation of Jesus' glory, his death on the cross (cf. Jn. 12:28-32) — they who had already drunk the Blood of the Lamb she was now offering for them. "Behold your son" would mean to Mary, "Give birth to Me again, Me, your Only-Begotten One, in this youngest one, by helping him to rediscover his faith in my Resurrection."

But the words of Jesus, "Behold your mother! Behold your son!" could also have a more directly Eucharistic significance for the primitive Church. These words fell upon John's ears on the very day after he had been ordained a priest of the New Covenant. In awe he had listened to Jesus' testament: "Do this in remembrance of me" (Lk. 22:19).[80] In direct obedience to this command, this sacred order, he would fulfill Mary's wish at Cana: "Do whatever he tells you" (Jn. 2:5). At the Last Supper he had become the servant and sacramental minister of the Messianic nuptials. Hearing Jesus say to him — a priest newly empowered to feed the Spouse of the Lamb, the Church — "Behold your mother," John would be enlightened by the Spirit after the Resurrection, (cf. Jn. 2:21; 16:12), if not at this moment. He would know that, henceforth, he must, as hierarchic mediator between the Son and the mother, at last fulfill, in all its plenitude, the command given at Cana. He must offer to his mother — Jesus' mother — the new wine of the Blood of the Only-Begotten Son.

During Jesus' public life no one had put such faith in the

---

80. I am adopting the translation proposed by Jeremias and P. de Broglie, and justified by J. Leguyer, *Le Sacrifice de la Nouvelle Alliance,* Mappus, Lyon, 1962, pp. 192-6.

prediction of the Bread of Life as did Mary. She, who had witnessed the miracle of the Incarnation in her virginal womb, now longed, as none other, for the Eucharist, that she might dwell in Jesus and have life (cf. Jn. 6:56-8). After the Resurrection, no one received with greater faith and love the Body and Blood of the One whom she had given to the world, so that He might give his flesh for the life of the world (cf. Jn. 6:51), the flesh he had received from her. In the days of the early Church the words "Behold your son!" meant to Mary: "The one was born of your faith at the time of the Annunciation, at Cana and beneath the cross, will represent Me; he will make Me present, very close to you. He will nourish you with my Flesh and Blood, your gift to Me, and thus I shall prepare you for a resurrection like my own" (cf. Jn. 6:51).

(Later still in the Church's history, after Mary's death and glorious Assumption, which are intimated in the Book of Revelation [11: 19; 12: 1, 6 and 14], the idea developed that the supremely meritorious Communions of the Immaculate One had merited resurrection for her *ex condigno,* as well as the privilege of an anticipated resurrection *de congruo.* But always, her Assumption was recognized first and foremost as a gratuitous gift of the Risen Jesus).[81]

"From that hour the disciple took her to his own home" (Jn. 19:27). Pere Braun has stressed the symbolic sense of this text.[82]

In the early Church every Christian was seen as "the disciple whom Jesus loved." Each one should, according to the explanation of Pope Leo XIII,[83] open his heart to Mary.

---

81. See the analysis of the teaching of St. Robert Bellarmine on this point by P.S. Tromp, *Marianum* XIII (1951), pp. 146-7; and my notes 98-99.
82. F.M. Braun, O.P., *La mere des Fideles,* Castermann, 1953, pp. 124-9.
83. Leo XIII, the encyclical *Augustissimae Virginis* of September 12, 1897: "Ingravescente aetate . . . facere non possumus quin omnibus et singulis

Offering hospitality to that heart which had been transfixed by the sword of his own sins, each one might also rejoice in the joy of the Co-redemptrix. By the expression "to his own home," is meant John's home, where he welcomed Mary, and this is a symbol of the Universal Church opening itself in faith to the heart of its mother.

John was not the only one to receive and welcome Mary; the whole primitive Church did this in a sense, offering her profound esteem and a love filled with gratitude. Together with the other members of the Church, Mary was "devoted . . . to the apostles' teaching and fellowship, to the breaking of the bread and the prayers day by day" (cf. Acts 2:42). To this day, at each Mass, Mary's heart is united with her Son's Blood in the Spirit. She offers the Father her tears and sufferings of the past and her love at the foot of the cross for the salvation of the entire world.

This is surely the reason why the Church welcomes its virginal mother so ardently during the celebration of the Holy Mysteries. Her nuptials with the Lamb are the central act in the life of the ecclesial community. The Church offers a loving welcome here, with her repeated plea for Mary's intercession during the Mass. She is imploring the intercession of the Mother of the Lamb.

I therefore affirm that the Church, in loving and venerating the heart of her mother, especially during the Holy Sacrifice, is loving her own ecclesial heart, wholly centered as this heart is upon the love of the Eucharist. She is glorifying and imitating the unspeakable earthly and

---

in Christo filiis nostris ipsius cruce pendentis extrema verba, quasi testamento relicta, iteremus: Ecce mater tua. Ac praeclare quidem nobiscum actum esse censebimus, si id nostrae commendationes effecerint ut unusquisque fidelis mariali cultu nihil habeat antiquius, nihil carius, liceatque de singulis usurpare verba Joannis, quae de se scripsit: 'Accepit eam discipulus in sua' " (Leo XIII, *Apostolic Letters,* B. Presse, Vol. V, p. 168).

heavenly love of the Theotokos for the Eucharist, and for the People of God whose unity is symbolized by the Eucharist. The hour of God's momentary powerlessness[84] on the Cross has passed; Mary's all-powerful prayer of intercession, offered close to the Lamb and in union with Him, lives on.

---

84. I adopt here the very remarkable and original interpretation, too little known and noticed by exegetes and theologians, given on the subject of the wedding of Cana by E. Testa, O.F.M., *Studii biblici franciscani,* Bk. V, Jerusalem, 1955, pp. 139-90, in particular pp. 184 ff. Jesus, in saying "My hour is not yet come" meant "the hour of darkness in which I shall work no miracles is not yet come (see Jn. 11:8-10), and so I can work the miracle which you ask of me." Refer also to the original interpretation of A. Kerrigan, O.F.M.: *De Mariologia et oecumenismo,* Rome, 1962, 71-119.

The Dying and Risen Heart of Mary, Paschal Heart of the Church

The heart of Mary, consoler, counsellor[85] and nurturer[86] of the Church, expanded in ever deepening love. After her Son's Passover this growth accelerated. Mary kept ever before her eyes "the features of Jesus Christ on the cross" (cf. Gal. 3:1). She beheld unceasingly in the Church the powerful effects of his Resurrection (cf. Eph. 3:20). Hers was ". . . a life of sorrow and of death....Love caused her to sorrow, and this sorrow brought her to the point of death; love came to her aid to make her live, so as to cause her sorrow to live as well....Always, she beheld Jesus Christ in agony on his cross, always the depths of her soul, and not merely her ears, were pierced by the last cry of her Well-Beloved as He died; a cry that was truly terrible and

---

85. See St. Irenaeus, *Demonstration of apostolic preaching,* No. 33; see the commentaries of P. D. Unger, O.F.M. Cap.: Iraenei doctrina de Maria socia Jesu in recapitulatione (*Maria et Ecclesia,* Roma, 1959, Vol. IV, pp. 85-91) on the phrase of St. Irenaeus: "Virgo virginis advocata." St. John Damascene (D. II, 8) calls Mary: "Our consolation," "emetera paraklesis."
86. The expression is St. Robert Bellarmine's, op. cit., Vol. II, p. 99; see *Marianum* 26 (1964), p. 367.

heart-breaking," as Bossuet says magnificently.[87]

Mary's immaculate heart, which had never merited death, died daily (I Cor. 15:31) out of love for Christ crucified. More truly than St. Paul could she say: "I have been crucified with Christ" (Gal. 2:19). The same love which caused her virginal heart to beat in unison with Christ's during his Passion, halted its beatings in a physical death at the very moment when, in an ultimate act of freedom, it had reached its highest peak. At the hour of her death Mary was "incomparably more filled with grace, more holy, more beautiful, more divinized than the greatest saints or the highest angels, taken singly or all together,"[88] — and also more filled with love.

The fact of Mary's death is a truth taught by the ordinary magisterium of the Church.[89] It is a truth rich in salvific import for the life of the People of God, one which the Church may even define solemnly, should she judge it opportune. For my present purposes I shall illustrate it with the help of the Byzantine liturgy and St. John Damascene.

The death of Mary's heart was like no other, for her death was privileged in its cause, its nature and its effects.

Its cause: "It is no cause for wonder that the virginal Co-redemptrix of the world should die, since the Creator of the world Himself died in the flesh."[90] It would not be fitting for Mary, a creature of Christ and redeemed by Him,

---

87. Bossuet, *Sermon II sur l'Assomption,* Point 1, Lebarcq, Vol. IV.
88. Discourse of Pius XII of May 13, 1946 (radio message to Fatima).
89. See J. Galot, S.J., *Maria,* VII, Beauchesne, 1964, which devotes twenty pages to the theological analysis of problems raised by the death of Mary, and then gives a full bibliography (191-211, 234-7). In the light of the "transitus" we must consider Mary's death as an historical fact (*Maria,* Vol. VI, pp. 135-145-6, 153).
90. Matins of the Assumption in the liturgy of the Byzantine rite: see the text in Mercenier, *Priere des Eglises du rite byzantin,* Amay, 1939, Vol. II, p. 303.

41

to be preserved from death. Mary is not God, but the Mother of God ". . . and had no part in the eternal birth of his divinity; we do not address her as a goddess — far from us be the deceptions of Greek fables — since indeed we proclaim her death." This is precisely why ". . . we know her as the Mother of the Incarnate God."[91] Mary's death confirms the historic character of Marian teaching, distant as it is from any form of Docetism. "She, the source of life, the Mother of my Lord, is dead! Yes, it must needs be that what was taken from earth should return to earth and by this road mount to heaven . . ."[92]

Its nature: "O incomparable passage of death, which wins you the grace of departing to God! For, if this grace is given by God to all his servants possessed of his spirit, the distance between the servants of God and his mother is infinite. What, then, shall we call this mystery which has been accomplished in you? Death? But if your holy and all-blessed soul is separated from your beauteous and immaculate body, and if this body is delivered to the tomb, still it does not linger in death, nor is it destroyed by corruption. For her sake whose virginity remained intact in her childbearing, her body is preserved from decomposition at the close of her life. It is placed within a better and more divine dwelling place which will last for a whole infinity of ages. Your body disappeared in death, yet through you, inexhaustible floods of immortal life spring up for us."[93] In a word, Mary's heart, a virginal heart, died, but did not know the corruption of the tomb.

---

91. St. John Damascene, D. II, II (V, 161-3). I was unable to consult the work of G. Chevalier, *La mariologie de S. J. Damascene,* Orient. Christ. Analecta, CIX, Rome, 1936.
92. St. John Damascene, D. III, 3 (V, 187).
93. St. John Damascene, D. I, 10 (V, 109). Damascene does not explicitly state, but seems to almost suggest, that it was through her very death that Mary caused the springs of immortality to flow forth for us.

How shall we portray the last moments of Mary? The Doctor of Damascus has done it with no less poetic splendor than theological depth. Here is the prayer which he places on the lips of Mary in her agony:

"Into your hands, my Son, I commend my spirit. Receive my soul, which is dear to You, and which You have preserved from all stain. To You, and not to earth, I return my body . . . Bring me close to You, to share your dwelling place. I hasten to return to You, Who came down to me annihilating all distance between us. As for my *well-beloved children,*[94] whom You were pleased to call your brethren,

---

94. Here we have two affirmations which seem clear to me regarding the spiritual motherhood of Mary. They seem to have escaped Msgr. Jouassard, perspicacious though he is; he only noticed what I mentioned in the second place (the first, in the text of the holy Doctor: D. II, 8). He translates the text elsewhere in such a way that he seems to conclude with a contradiction: "do not leave us orphans, exposed to danger, You, the Mother of your Son full of sympathy" and he may thus conclude that the idea of spiritual maternity is absent, on the explicit plane, in Damascene (Etudes Mariales, *Maternite spirituelle de Marie,* I, Lethielleux, 1959, p. 78). The translation of P. Voulet, which I have used, seems to me much closer to the original Greek. On the one hand if the Apostles, addressing the dying Mary, begged her to remain with them, praying her not to leave them orphans, and then immediately afterwards call her their Mother, it seems as if they considered her as their Mother (in the eyes of Damascene). On the other hand, the word "pro-kinduneuo" is in the genitive and remains thus in Msgr. Jouassard's translation. The translation of P. Voulet, which came later, (it appeared in 1962) therefore seems more faithful to me. In a more general way it seems that a serious study of the theological content of "transitus" (see *Maria,* VI, 733-156, the brilliant study of Cothenet) would lead one to perceive that the affirmation of spiritual maternity is already contained in these very early accounts, precisely in the description of the death of Mary. Voulet (op. cit., p. 30) shows with what discernment St. John Damascene used them in connection with the death of Mary. Why not the same in regard to his teaching on the spiritual maternity of Mary? Finally, I note that the supplication reported by Damascene in D.II, 8 (see the text quoted in footnote 89) is addressed to the Mother of God

do You console them Yourself for my departure. Add a new blessing to those which they already enjoy, through the imposition of my hands.''

But the pilgrim Church, Damascene thinks, wishes to keep Mary: '''Stay with us, you who are our consolation, our sole comfort on this earth. Do not leave us orphans, *O Mother; we face danger for the sake of your compassionate Son. Allow us to keep you as our solace in pain, as refreshment in our labors! If you depart, you who are God's dwelling place, let us go with you, for we are called *your people* on account of your Son. In you, we possess the sole consolation left to us on this earth. We will rejoice to live with you if you live, or to follow you in death if you die! But what have we said — 'if you die'? For you, death itself is life, and a better life, incomparably preferable to this present life. For us, though, would life still be life if we were deprived of your company?' Such were the words,'' concludes St. John Damascene, ''which the Apostles, *with the whole assembly of the Church,* addressed to the Blessed Virgin.''[95]

We grasp the thought underlying this magnificent lyricism; the Church of all times, daughter of Mary and her people because it is the People of God in Jesus Christ, ought to gather mystically around the deathbed and then around the tomb of his mother,[96] to die to the world with her and to

---

not only by the Apostles but also by ''the crowd of saints who surrounded her, living in their bodies.'' This, perhaps, and notwithstanding Jouassard (op. cit., p. 77, note 96) is not an apocryphal creation, rather their affirmation of an ecclesial tradition, like that ''very ancient account [of the death of Mary] which has been handed down to us from father to son'' (St. John Damascene, D. II, 4). See A. Rivera, in *Ephemerides Mariologicae,* 1957, pp. 359 ff.

95. St. John Damascene, D. II, 8-9 (V, 145-7).

96. The Doctor of Damascus ends his last homily on Mary's death and Assumption, which he gave at Gethsemani before the Virgin's tomb when

return to God. The dialogue with the heart of Mary, agonizing in love, is a part of the structure of ecclesial life. How could the children of Mary not be present at the death of their mother? It is for this reason, as we shall detail below,[97] that we would like to see the Vigil of the Assumption transformed into the Dormition of Mary in the Latin rite — a feast already existing in the Coptic rite.

I further perceive, in the symbol of Mary's blessing, the lived consciousness that Mary did not abandon the world when dying, and this is clearly expressed in the Byzantine liturgy: "In your motherhood you preserved your virginity; at the time of your Dormition you did not abandon the world, O Mother of God; you have been transferred to Life, you, the Mother of Life, and through your intercession you deliver our souls from death."[98] What is missing, however, in the great thought of the Eastern Christian regarding Mary's death, is the concept of Mary offering up her death in union with the Passion of her Son for the salvation of

---

he was already very old and his own tomb seemed to open up at his feet, with this astonishing development: "All of you, let us leave this world in spirit with her who has gone before. Yes, all of you, with heart's desire, accompanying the one who went down into the tomb, let us go down too! . . . Let us surround the immaculate tomb and draw upon divine grace. Come, let us embrace her in spirit and carry her ever virginal body! Let us enter the sepulchre; let us die with her, casting off the passions of the body but living with her a life without worldly desires, without stain." (D. III, 52; V, 193-5). And Damascene compares the tomb of Mary "full of glory" to a "marriage chamber" whence she will rise up to the wedding feast, "after having bequeathed her tomb itself like a nuptial couch to those who remain upon this earth," who will have "not bodily union but the life of holy souls, that is to say, near God, a condition better and sweeter than any other" (D. III, 2). In other words, the Church on earth gathers around Mary's tomb as around the nuptial bed of her union with God.

97. See Appendix.
98. Mercenier, op. cit., Vol. II, p. 295.

the world — the concept of her co-sacrificial death.

Damascene does speak elsewhere, in passing, of the effects of Mary's death: "By no means does death render you happy; it is you who have shed a splendor upon death; you have scattered its sadness and shown that it is a joy.[99] Mary's death, like a sun, illumines our own; she communicates to it her own joy. For the one who has "broken the bonds of death," death shall be "a bridge leading to life, a passage to immortality."[100]

St. John Damascene affirms the resurrection of Mary, as does the Byzantine liturgy, and this serves to emphasize once more her physical death: "It was necessary that her flesh, after casting off its earthly, opaque weight of mortality, should be purified like gold in the crucible of death, and then arise from the tomb clothed in all the brilliance of incorruptibility."[101] "Your death brings you to a truly divine and everlasting life, O Immaculate One, where you contemplate your Son and Lord in joy," comments the Byzantine liturgy.[102]

The heart of Mary, whose beating was stilled through love for mortal men, beats anew in purest love for all humanity now that she is gloriously risen. We can apply to her heart what St. John Damascene says magnificently of her body: this maternal and virginal heart is "the source of all resurrection" (*to tes panton anastaseos aition*).[103]

In Damascene's thought the Assumption represents a spiritual and corporeal glorification, following upon the merits of Mary's Immaculate Heart. It represents a spiritual glorification first of all. He puts this prayer for Mary on

---

99. St. John Damascene, D. I, 12 (V, 115).
100. Ibid., D. II, 8 (V, 145).
101. Ibid., D. III, 3 (V, 187).
102. Mercenier, op. cit., Vol. II, p. 301.
103. St. John Damascene, D. III, 4 (V, 189).

the lips of the Church before her death: "Come down, come down, O Sovereign Lord, come and *pay your mother the reward she merited* for having nourished you! Open your divine hands: receive her maternal *soul,* You Who on the cross returned your spirit into the hands of the Father. Address a sweet invitation to her: You shared everything with Me; come, enjoy with Me all that I have."[104]

The Assumption represents a corporeal glorification too, for the merits of the compassionate Virgin — "She [Mary] should be raised from the tomb, the mother should be united with her Son....She who contemplated her Son on the cross and received in her heart (egkardion) the sword of sorrow which she had been spared in giving birth to Him must needs contemplate Him seated at the Father's hand."[105]

It is clear, therefore, that the heart of Mary has merited, with a merit of fittingness, her own privileged glorification in the mystery of the Assumption. The Doctor of Damascus, who is perhaps more the poet and chanter of Mary's loving death than of her glorious resurrection, seems to experience something of the compassion of medievals before the sorrows of Mary standing at the foot of the cross, as he dwells upon the death of the Mother of God. He cannot conceive that the Church should not gather in a grief at once sad and joyful to celebrate the last beating of the mortal heart of the Immaculate One and the first beating of her immortal and risen heart.

In his view, as is sufficiently clear from the above quotations, Mary's heart died and is risen as the heart of the Church. She died on account of and for the sins of men, and was raised for their justification, that she might intercede physically for them (cf. Rom. 4:25; Heb. 9:24). Mary died

---

104. Ibid., D. III, 4 (V, 191).
105. Ibid., D. II, 14, (V, 159).

not for herself but for the Lord, belonging in her death to the Lord Jesus, her Savior. She died and has returned to life to rule over the living and the dead (cf. Rom. 14:7-9). "She died for all, so that the living might no longer live for themselves, but for her who died and is risen for their sakes" (cf. II Cor. 5:15).

To all, Mary can say: "Make room for me in your hearts . . . you are in my heart in life and in death" (cf. II Cor. 7: 2-3). The glorious resurrection of the heart of Mary is, as Father Schillebeeckx so well said in speaking of the Assumption, ". . . the climax of Mary's redemption. It emphasizes once more the unique character of her privileged role in the distribution of the fruits of the Redemption. "Mary," to quote the Dominican theologian again, "participates by her Assumption in the power of Jesus as Lord." Her resurrection is for her the "coming into power" of her motherhood of men (cf. Rom. 1:4). The Virgin's queenship is the glorious fruit of her own redemption and of her collaboration in ours; she participates in the glorification of her Son reigning at the right hand of the Father as Redeemer of Mary and of the world.[106]

---

106. Schillebeeckx, op. cit., pp. 82-3 and 96-7. The last thoughts of Schillebeeckx evoke a text of St. Irenaeus perhaps not sufficiently studied: "It was necessary and fitting to bring Adam to completion in Christ, so that what was mortal might be caught up into immortality, and Eve in Mary" (*Adv. Haer.* III, 22, 3-4). I wonder if this text does not suggest Mary's resurrection and Assumption, like the glory of Jesus. In this case it would be one of the most ancient traditional witnesses to it.

PART II

The Immaculate Heart of Mary
Peerless Member
And
Heart of the Church

I have lingered too long, and at the same time I have moved too swiftly over the light thrown upon the whole of Marian dogma by Mary's heart. I say this in view of a deeper understanding of the place of that heart in the very center of the mystery of Christ and the Church.

It seems fitting, therefore, to take a closer look now, on the theological level, at the relationship between the cult the Church gives to Mary's heart and Mary's pre-eminence as the heart of the Church. I shall emphasize the ecumenical and pastoral advantages accruing to this, so as to better grasp all the ecclesial significance attaching to the consecration to the Immaculate Heart of Mary.

The Meaning of the Expression "Heart of Mary" For the Magisterium

To my knowledge there has been to date only one document of the Magisterium giving a precise meaning to the expression "Heart of Mary." It is the Decree of the Congregation of Rites of May 4, 1944, on the liturgical cult of the Immaculate Heart of Mary, "symbol of the sublime and unsurpassed sanctity of the soul of the Mother of God, and above all of her ardent love for God and his Son, Jesus Christ, as well as her maternal devotedness to men purchased with his divine Blood."[107] There still remains a bit of uncertainty, however, as in the case of the exact text of the Office of the Immaculate Heart of Mary approved by Pope Pius XII. In that instance the pope did not say that he approved the ideas developed in the paragraph entitled "Urbis et Orbis."[108] The Decree of the Congregation of Rites mentioned above leaves a doubt as to whether it is

---

107. AAS 37 (1945) 50. The translation is borrowed from G. Geenen, O.P., author of the article: "Historical and doctrinal antecedents of the consecration of the world to the Immaculate Heart of Mary," *Maria,* I, 827-73.
108. AAS 37 (1945) 51.

presenting a definite stand of the Magisterium as such.

However this may be, even were the answer in the affirmative, this definition by no means exhausts the subject, and would not prevent the Magisterium from defining the object of the cult given by the Church to the Immaculate Heart of Mary in more precise terms if it judged it opportune. The example of precisions brought to bear on the definition of the exact object of the cult offered to the Heart of Jesus in the encyclical *Haurietis Aquas* is there for us to remember. We note especially that the definition of the "Heart of Mary" of 1944 makes no allusion to the divine Persons, in particular to the Holy Spirit, nor to angelic persons. It is also clear that Mary's love for men is envisaged under the aspect of the redeeming love, of which they are themselves the object. In other words, it emphasizes Mary's maternal and merciful love for men who are loved by the redeeming love of her Son and their Brother, Jesus Christ. Finally, I note that this definition makes no explicit allusion to Mary's love for the Church, or for the creative and redeeming love of God.

Theologians and the Expression "Mary, Heart of the Church"

The earliest expression of this concept-image, as far as we know at present, would be the one left to us by the Franciscan Servasanctus of Faenza (d. 1300), better known by the name of Ernest of Prague, the name he used to sign the "Mariale." On account of her unshakeable faith throughout the Passion, he calls Mary "the heart of the Church" (heart of the Spouse or Church), which watched for the whole body on Holy Saturday when Christ slept in the tomb. Then, the other members of the Church having failed, she herself, like the heart, remained as the life of the body ("the life of the body remained in her alone as in the heart").[109]

Ernest of Prague was obviously referring to the Song of Songs (5:2) where the spouse says, "I sleep, but my heart watches." It is likely that further research into medieval commentaries on the Song would bring to light other expressions of the idea of Mary, heart of the Church (see song 3:1). The Marian sense of medieval commentaries on the Song of Songs has already often been explored, but has it always been from this point of view? I might adduce here

---

109. Binder, *Maria et Ecclesia,* III, 427; see Dillenschneider, op. cit., 283.

the remark of the May 4, 1944, decree already cited, which points out that "distant traces of the liturgical cult of the Immaculate Heart of Mary can be found in the commentaries of the Fathers of the Church on the spouse of the Song of Songs."[110]

Next, in the nineteenth century the expression "Mary, heart of the Church" reappeared in the texts of German Catholic theologians, and in the twentieth century in Russian Sophianic Mariology.

Scheeben, although he does not consider all its aspects, is incontestably its most powerful theologian and popularizer. He has developed its meaning at length, as some of our citations make clear, even permitting his own relationship with the cult of the Immaculate Heart of Mary to enter into his discussion. In the text which I already quoted at the beginning of this book,[111] he places these two notions alongside one another rather than coordinating or synthesizing them. It is to him, however, that we are indebted for the basic intuition of this work: If the heart of Mary is "the vital center of her person" and "as such represents her," and on the other hand, Mary is "the mystical heart of the Mystical Body of Christ," it is not difficult to conclude that the Immaculate Heart of Mary is the heart of the Church.

Beyond these logical connections, however, profound reasons for this identification flow from the most synthetic and systematic exposition of the basis for calling Mary the Heart of the Church. S. Tromp, S.J. has given us these reasons with a quite special authority. It seems that his point of departure was a reaction against the difficulties he encountered in the expression "Holy Spirit, Heart of the

---

110. AAS 37 (1945) 50.
111. See Footnote 2.

Church," twice used by St. Thomas Aquinas.[112]

I shall quote him in summary:

Mary's influence in the life of the Church, considered as a saving institution, is affective. Mary's great power lies in her maternal love, with its symbol of the tender heart of a human person."

After having stressed the fact that Christ is the Head of the Body, consubstantial with this body through the materiality of his human nature, and that the Holy Spirit is its purely spiritual and immaterial soul (a reason why it would be better to avoid the image of the heart), Tromp continues:

"The heart is on the one hand a material organ, and on the other hand it sends a continuous, hidden stream of life coursing through the body, all the more intense for being inspired by love.

"In consequence, since Mary is a human person like us, and since she collaborates in a hidden way in our supernatural life of grace, she can and *should* be called the heart of the Mystical Body. She collaborates in our supernatural life in a pre-eminent way because she embraces us in maternal love. Under the impulse of this love she spreads throughout the entire social and supernatural Body of Christ, streams of grace reddened with his blood, even as in former times the tenderness of her motherly heart caused the blood of her virginal womb to flow through the newly incarnate members of the Word."[113]

---

112. St. Thomas Aquinas, *de Ver.* 29, 4, 7: "Cor est membrum latens, caput autem patens"; *Summa Theologiae* III, 8, 11, 3: "caput habet manifestam eminentiam . . . sed cor habet quandam influentiam occultam." See Tromp, *De spiritu Christi anima,* Rome, Gregorienne, 1960, pp. 33-5.

113. Tromp, op. cit., pp. 181-2 *"Evidens est* cur B. Virgo Maria quae inter sanctos non solum eminet sed habet inter eos locum omnino transcendentem, *dici* possit ac *debeat* Cor Mystici Corporis": and the

Tromp then emphasizes the fact that unlike the soul, the heart is not present in every part of the body, nor does it give it its unity or vivify it an an ultimate life principle.[114] For these reasons the image of the heart is seen to be inferior to that of the soul, and he concludes:

"In light of all this, it seems that the image of heart ought to be applied to the Mother of God rather than to the Paraclete. Due to her humanity the Virgin is consubstantial with us and with Christ the Head. Her place in the Church is central, yet invisible. Through her intercession and mediation she brings about the distribution of grace and gifts through the entire Mystical Body. Finally, as St. John Chrysostom puts it so well, the heart can act only if it receives direction and movement from the head, and in the same way the Virgin can do all she does only through the power of Christ.[115] The heart is the symbol of love, which is the ultimate basis of the intercession of the Mother of God."[116]

These considerations of the eminent theologian of the Mystical Body of Christ seem to me solidly and substantially founded. All that he says about *Mary* as the heart of the Church can be applied still more precisely to Mary's *heart*. This is no more than to explain the thought of Tromp and Scheeben, rendering their images more vigorous and enlightening by intensifying them. Here we find applied to the case of Mary the very biblical and patristic "theology

---

Dutch theologian cites an article in which he has given a detailed exposition of this view: "Die Sendung Mariens und das geheimnis der Kirche," *Theologie und Glaube,* 1953, pp. 401-412. Unfortunately I have not been able to find it. He adds: "imago Mariae ut est collum Ecclesiae non solum minus elegans est, sed insuper minus exprimit exprimenda."

114. St. Thomas Aquinas, *Summa Theologiae* I, 75, 1: the heart is a principle but not the ultimate principle of the life of the body.

115. St. John Chrysostom, on Eph. Ch. 4, hom. 11, 4: MG 62, 84-5.

116. Tromp, op. cit., 208-10.

of images" of which D. Clement Lialine recently noted a brilliant application in the encyclical *Mystici Corporis*.[117]

---

117. Irnikon, commentary of D. Lialine on *Mystici corporis* shortly after its appearance, in 1946-1947.

Mary, Heart of the Church
In Russian Sophianic Mariology

Russian Sophianic Mariology, despite certain presuppositions and conclusions which the Catholic Church cannot adopt, gives a brilliant and stimulating example of this theology of images extolled by the Russian Benedictine monk. In it the theme of Mary, heart of the Church, is central.

Soloviev, founder of this school, inspired at once by Platonism and German Idealism, wrote: "The body dies only when smitten in its two essential parts, head and heart. But the head and heart of the Church — Christ and Mary — live in the eternity of God and are invulnerable."[118]

In our century Paul Florenskij (b. 1881) wrote: "If the Lord is the head of the Church, sweet Mary, dispenser of the divine bounty, is truly the heart, through which the Church communicates to its members life, eternity and the gifts of the Spirit, for she is the true source of life . . . the only center of the Church's life."[119]

---

118. V. Soloviev, *Fondaments spirituels de la vie,* Beauchesne, Paris, 1932, p. 174.
119. See B. Schultze, S.J. "Mariologie sophianique russe," *Maria,* VI, p. 225. The adjective "exclusive" perhaps marks the rejection of a visible center.

57

It is above all Bulgakov, however, who has insisted upon our theme. Father B. Schultze, S.J. sums up the thought of the Russian theologian as follows:

"Mary is the heart of the Church, she is in some sort its personification; and inasmuch as she is the personification of the Church, the Mother of God is raised beyond all sin. She is the living heart of the Church and its personal authority. She is the heart of the world and the spiritual center of all humanity. While she lived in this world it was not one of the apostles — not Peter, not John — but Mary who was the living heart of the Church, its center, the supreme and incontestable personal authority, and this became still more apparent after her death."[120] Bulgakov even thinks that the Apostle John, because he was called the son (of Mary) by the crucified Christ, "received the primacy of the Apostles," a primacy distinct from that of Peter and equally divine in its origin.[112]

These very suggestive reflections call for the following commentaries:

1. It is very true to say that Mary personifies the Church, but as its transcendant type, as a cause not only exemplary but also efficient (although dependent). It is precisely because Mary personifies the Church as a communion of love that she can and should be called its heart, and Mary's heart, which personifies Mary, should be called the heart of the Church. And since the Church is itself the *raison d'etre* of the universe, as St. Epiphanius said,[122] Mary can also be

---

120. Schultze, op. cit., pp. 234 and 233.
121. Ibid., *Maria et Ecclesia,* V. X, Rome, 1960: "Maria und Kirche in der russischen Sophia-Theologie," p. 94. He cites the work of Bulgakov on Peter and John.
122. St. Epiphanius, *Adv. Haer.* I, 5; MG 41 181 B.

called the heart of humanity and of the world.

2. As Father Schultze demonstrates, applying the image of the heart to Mary's place in the Church has the advantage of emphasizing her active role.[123] Her role in the Church is not purely passive, as Barth would have it. Bulgakov, however, minimizes Mary's passivity.

The most serious criticism I can make is that unconsciously he has transferred to Mary the supreme juridical authority in the Church, denying it to Peter. After ignoring it in Peter's regard on the visible plane, he affirms it gratuitously for Mary in the primitive Church, and now that Mary is in heaven he reduces this supreme authority to something purely invisible. He thus eliminates the visibility of the Church![124]

In reality Peter was already the visible head of the Church during Mary's life, after the Ascension of Jesus. Mary was subject to him, as formerly she had been to Joseph. Mary's hidden but very real influence upon the primitive Church functioned like that of the heart in the human body, invisibly, through prayer and love. Already Mary was the invisible heart of the visible Church. This invisible influence had visible repercussions and was coupled with a visible influence through word and example. Today Mary is not only the invisible heart of the visible Church but also its invulnerable heart in every sense of the word, and this heart becomes in some sort visible in and through the loving prayer of the Church, virgin and mother.

---

123. Schultze, *Maria et Ecclesia,* X, loc. cit., p. 64.

124. See Pius XII, *Mystici Corporis Christi*: "Sublato enim adspectabili hoc Capite, as diffractis conspicuis unitatis vinculis mysticum Redemptoris corpus ita obscurant ac deformant ut ab aeternae quaerentibus salutis portum iam nec videri, neque inveniri queat" (AAS 35 (1943) 211). See the affirmation of Denis the Carthusian: "Principi Apostolorum tamquam totius Ecclesiae praelato [Maria] fuit humillime subdita" (*In cant*. 8, 26).

Actually, Scheeben had answered Bulgakov in advance:
"In the Mystical Body of Christ Mary's place is most fully defined as the heart....Mary thus appears as the member in which all the life of the head is most perfectly reflected, the member whose functions condition and sustain the head's action on the other members in multiple ways. Moreover, this image shows in a striking manner Mary's personal and vibrant role in the interior organism of the Body of Christ, as contrasted with the role redounding to Christ's official representatives in the external organism of the Church....Mary has no part in the exercise of the public power of the Magisterium or of royalty (Scheeben is alluding here to the power of jurisdiction). Her collaboration with Christ is rather the intimate and secret collaboration of the heart with the head in the *interior* communication of life to the members, an activity through which Christ supremely fulfills his mission of Redeemer.[125]

Thus Mary's role in the Church is greater than Peter's — an external ministry — or John's. It is basically different and complementary. Catholic Mariology, in defining Mary's role as heart of the Church, avoids both the errors-by-defect of Protestantism and the errors-by-excess of the Russian Sophianic school. Obviouly the Catholic Church, while denying to Mary Peter's juridical power over the Church, affirms her royal sway over the People of God who are also her people, and her full right to be known, praised and loved.

---

125. Scheeben, op. cit., pp. 112-2; 168. On this theme of the heart of Mary in some way visible in and through the loving prayer of the Church, see Scheeben again: "Her [Mary's] prayer in the midst of the Apostles while awaiting the Holy Spirit contains in particular, and for all times, the type of relationship found in regard to Mary of the Church, mediating the grace of Redemption. This relationship does not consist merely in the fact that the Church is animated and sustained by Mary's prayer. It consists quite specially in this, that *the Church's prayer asking for the fruits of Redemption is animated and sustained by the prayer of Mary the heart of the Church*" (op. cit. p. 199). Scheeben is giving us a beautiful interpretation of Acts 1:14.

Mary, Heart of the Church, And the Proclamation of Her Ecclesial Motherhood by Paul VI

Some readers may object that the Church has just solemnly proclaimed that Mary is her mother through the voice of Pope Paul VI, without alluding to her fuction as heart.

It is certainly true that there is no text of the Magisterium, to my knowledge, that states explicitly that Mary is the heart of the Church. Still, in the very discourse in which Paul VI proclaimed Mary, Mother of the Church, and made it clear that this title ''synthesizes admirably the privileged place of the Virgin in the Holy Church, recognized by this Council (Vatican II),''[126] he also recalled that Mary is ''the best part, the loftiest, most noble, most favored'' member of the Church. Most importantly, he solemnly promulgated the Dogmatic Constitution *Lumen Gentium*. This latter affirms, in the same phrase where it implies that Mary is its mother (''the Catholic Church honors her with filial affection and piety as a most beloved mother''), that Mary is also its ''pre-eminent and altogether singular member.''[127]

---

126. Paul VI, discourse of Nov. 21, 1964, AAS 56 (1964), 1.015. I use the translation of *Documentation catholique*.
127. LG, 53.

These two images, far from being in opposition, complement each other — which is not to say that they have an identical meaning. If we think of the Church as the family of God, we will call Mary its mother; if we think of it as the Mystical Body of Christ, then we say she is its heart. If we want to stress the fact that she is a member of the body, what other member would she be?[128] If we want to indicate her transcendence in relation to the other members of the body and her role as origin of the entire body, we will call her its mother.

Actually these two images, as they are being used with their precise connotations, seem to point to the same meaning. Mary is the mother of the Church because she is first of all its daughter as a creature of Christ, the head of the Church, and as ransomed by Him. She is "a daughter of Adam, she is our sister, a disciple of Christ, wholly ordered to God and to Christ, our sole Redeemer."[129] On the other hand, the theologians (Scheeben, Tromp) who exalt Mary as the heart of the Church also emphasize the fact that she is its mother.[130] And Father Schillebeeckx gives a

---

128. The image of the neck, used by St. Bernard and many medieval authors, besides presenting other difficulties (see footnote 107), does not express Mary's active role in the Church as does the image of the heart, nor does it symbolize Mary as "Mother of love" (an expression of the same St. Bernard, see note 67). The two images could be complementary, that of the neck showing more clearly that Mary joins humanity to the Word of Life.

129. Paul VI, Discourse of Nov. 21, 1964, op. cit., pp. 1016-7. Here he also quotes St. Ambrose: "sit in singulis Mariae anima ut magnificat Dominum; sit in singulis spiritus Mariae ut exsultet in Deo" (in Lk. 2, 26; ML 15, 1642). Here Ambrose was already developing the thought which Bossuet was to comment on later (see footnote 72).

130. See, among others, Schillebeeckx, op cit., pp. 121, 128-9; Scheeben, op. cit., p. 201.

marvelous exposition of the bond between the two images:

"As mother, type of the Church, [Mary] collaborates maternally in the building up of the Church undertaken by Christ. She is the mother of the Church, and this gives her her unique maternal character. But within this Church she is the spiritual-corporeal womb. As mother, she gives it life."[131]

The image of womb corresponds to that of heart, whose active and dynamic character we have already noted.

As Mary is the spiritual daughter of Jesus, head of the Church, only in order to be the mother of its members, she receives, as heart, the influx of the head so as to give blood and life to the other members.

On the speculative level nothing, absolutely nothing here is contrary to an eventual teaching of the Magisterium of the Church, who, after having solemnly proclaimed that Mary is at one and the same time a pre-eminent member and the Mother of the Church, might make it clear that her immaculate heart is the heart of the Church.

Regarding the title "Mary, Heart of the Church," we can say exactly what Paul VI said about the title "Mother of the Church": "It synthesizes admirably the privileged role of the Virgin in the Holy Church which was recognized by the Council." And when the titles are joined they demonstrate more clearly than when isolated, to use Pope Paul VI's expressions once more, how "the reality of the Church is not exhausted in its hierarchical structure, its liturgy, sacraments and juridical ordinances. Its profound essence and the primary source of its sanctifying efficacy are found in its mystical union with Christ, a union we cannot conceive of apart from her who is the Mother of the

---

131. Schillebeeckx, op. cit., pp. 128-9.

Word Incarnate."[132] Since the profound essence of the Church lies in its mystical union with Christ it is obvious that no one could realize it and incarnate it better than Mary, inseparably united to Jesus as heart to head.

---

132. Paul VI, Discourse of Nov. 21, 1964, op. cit., p. 1014.

Ecumenical and Pastoral Advantages Of the Presentation of The Immaculate Heart of Mary As Heart of the Church

With Vatican II the Catholic Church has entered upon a period of intense renewal. It is, therefore, normal that devotions which are rightly dear to Christians should be adapted to the present needs of the People of God and of all humanity. As its main doctrinal objective, the Council chose a deeper penetration into the mystery of the Church. It seems, therefore, that anything that might throw into clearer relief the relationship between this mystery and a devotion would be moving in the same direction as the breathings of the Spirit of Christ.

To present the heart of Mary as the heart of the Church is to associate visibly, in the hearts of Christians, two inseparable loves. It is to perceive reality more clearly, to unite two truths which the Council wished to consider together.

Also, in view of the Protestant tendency to subjectivity, it renders the acceptance of Marian dogma more acceptable, or at least more easy to comprehend. Again, it avoids offending the Protestant world by isolating Mary, a tendency with which we have been reproached.

Finally, it would facilitate reunion with the Orthodox Christians, many of whom, as we have said, love to think of Mary as the heart of the church. Would not devotion to the heart of Mary be more accessible to them if it were presented as devotion to the Heart of the Church?

I quote here an Orthodox Russian theologian[133] whom I have not yet mentioned: Mary is "the mystical heart of the Church, its mystical center, its perfection already realized in a human person fully united to God, beyond the Resurrection and judgment," writes V. Lossky.

Protestants and Orthodox Churchmen of good faith already belong in a certain way to the People of God[134] who are also, as St. John Damascene has made clear, the People of Mary.

This whole People of Mary aspires, consciously or unconsciously, to consecrate itself ever more perfectly to the service of the heart of its queen, which is also its own heart as the People of God, the triumphant heart of the pilgrim Church. This consecration is a stage in its historical pilgrimage. It is a new factor in the unification of the wayfaring People of God who, if they have a visible head to represent their invisible head, Jesus, have no other visible heart than the saints to represent, in some sense, their invisible heart, who is Mary.[135]

---

133. V. Lossky, *Theologie Mystique de l'Eglise d'Orient*, Paris, 1944, p. 190.

134. Decree of Vatican Council II "Unitatis redintegratio" on ecumenism; see No. 2. "Uni nempe collegio apostolico cui Petrus praeest credimus Dominum commisisse omnia bona Foederis Novi, ad constituendum unum Christi corpus in terris, cui plene incorporentur oportet omnes, qui ad populum Dei iam aliquo modo pertinent."

135. To illustrate Scheeben's text quoted in footnote 119, and in a general way our entire subject, I quote this fine extract from *The Story of a Soul* by St. Therese of the Child Jesus: "Pondering on the Mystical Body of

"Mary," says St. Peter Chrysologus, "received salvation in order to pass it on to succeeding ages"[136] and to human history. "This name of Mother of God," declares St. John Damascene, "contains the whole mystery of the Incarnation and the entire history of the divine economy in this world."[137]

To put it another way, the name of Mother of God contains all the history of the People of God in this world, the People of God who are and should be, through their

---

Holy Church, I could not recognize myself in any of the members described by St. Paul, or rather, I should have liked to see myself in all of them. Love gave me the key to my vocation. I understood that if the Church had a body composed of different members, the most important, the noblest of all organs was not lacking to her; I understood that she had a heart, and that this heart was on fire with love; I understood that love alone could send the members into action, that if love were extinguished apostles would not proclaim the Gospel, martyrs would refuse to shed their blood. I understood that love included all vocations, that love was everything and embraced all times and places, because it is eternal! . . . In an excess of rapturous joy I cried out: I have found my place in the heart of the Church, and this is the place which you, O my God, have given me: in the heart of my Mother the Church, I will be love! Thus I shall be everything; and so my dream will come true!" (*The Story of a Soul*, Ch. XI). In the visible Church the saints are at once invisible (no one perhaps could be completely certain of the holiness of another wayfarer) and visible (their works shine before men for the glory of their heavenly Father), and their holy love, drawn from the heart of Mary, heart of the Church, represents in an imperfect way Mary's pure love for the human race. The saints better than anyone else have recognized the duty of paying homage to this merciful and co-redeeming love, and consequently to the heart of Mary, symbol of the entire mystery of the Mother of God our Savior (see by analogy the Encyclical *Haurietis Aquas* of Pius XII: AAS 48 (1956), pp. 315-6 and 336). They know too, that they could never love the overflowing love of the Immaculate One for the human race sufficiently!

136. "Accepit Virgo salutem saeculis redditura" (*Sermo* 143, Latin Patrology, Migne 52, 5836).

137. St. John Damascene, *De fide orthodoxa*, III, 12; MG 94, 1029-32.

consecration to their queen, the People of Mary, so as to be fully and perfectly the People of God. For in consecrating themselves to Mary, heart of the Church, are they not consecrating themselves to the accomplishment of the will of the Immaculate Heart of Mary, which is the completion of the upbuilding of the Church, that Church which they themselves are?

The Meaning of the Consecration
To the Heart of Mary

Is this not what St. John Damascene was groping after obscurely? Not only did the great Marian homilist never tire of speaking of the Mother of the Word Incarnate — "What is there to offer to the Mother of the Word, if not our word?"[138] He drew from his own mystical Marian experience an ever stronger desire for total consecration to the Immaculate One. "What is there sweeter than the Mother of my God? She has captivated my spirit, she reigns over my tongue, day and night her image is before me. She, the Mother of the Word, provides me also with words to speak."[139] The former official of the caliphate, become a monk at the age of fifty, knew this from personal experience. "If we avoid our former vices with courage, if we love virtue with all our heart, she [Mary] will multiply her visits to us her own servants, bringing with her all good things; and she will bring us Christ, her royal Son and universal Lord, who will dwell in our hearts."[140]

If we want to help all Christians to taste the sweetness

---

138. Ibid., D. II, 1 (V, 125).
139. Ibid., D. III, 1, (V, 181).
140. Ibid., D. II, 19 (V, 177).

that is Mary, present day and night to their spirits, if we long for her to captivate their minds and rule over their speech, so that through her them may receive Christ's visits, let us renew our consecration to the heart of Mary, the immaculate heart of the immaculate Church. Hers is the virginal, nuptial and maternal heart of the Church, which is in turn virgin, spouse and mother. Her heart was redeemed in advance, that she might be the unique Co-redemptrix of the Church, the distributor of the fruits of the Redemption. Her heart, dead and resurrected, is the heart of that Church which is the spouse of the Lamb who created all things. Hers is the triumphant heart of the pilgrim Church, that Church which claims Mary as its mother, queen and handmaid.

We ought to take special inspiration from the words and example of St. John Damascene, author of one of the first acts of consecration to Mary:

"O Lady, Mother of God and Virgin, our hearts cling to you, our hope, as to an absolutely firm and unshakeable anchor. We consecrate to you our spirit, our soul, our body, each one of us in his entire person. We desire to honor you with psalms, hymns and inspired canticles (cf. Eph. 5:19; Col. 3:16) as far in us lies: for to honor you in the measure of your worth is beyond our power. If it is true, as we read in Sacred Scripture, that the honor paid to fellow servants is a proof of love for a common master, how can we fail to honor you, the Mother of *our* Master? Should we not seek this eagerly? Is it not worth more than our very life's breath, and does it not engender life? This is how we shall strengthen our attachment to our own Master. What am I saying? Truly it is enough for those who hold you in loving memory to have the inestimable gift of your remembrance. This will fill us with imperishable joy. What bliss fills that man, what blessings, when he has made of his soul *the secret dwelling place of your most holy remembrance!*"[141]

---

141. Ibid., D. I. 14, (V, 119).

Epilogue[1]

The present study, composed in Brazil in 1965, has been enriched by my experience of the deep love of the people of Latin America for the Immaculate Virgin.

In the course of numerous sojourns at the Catholic University of Portugal, at Lisbon and at Fatima, while teaching and making pilgrimages, I have been privileged to contemplate Portugal's veneration for the Immaculate Heart of Mary.

Kneeling in spirit before the graves of the Servants of God, Jacinta and Francisco Marto, I beg them to obtain for my readers a share in their contemplation of the mystery of Mary in the heart of the mystery of the Church, mysteries which have not been revealed not to the wise and learned but to little ones, indeed very little ones, through the mercy of the Father and the Son.

I therefore invite my readers to reflect with me upon several impressive papal texts which I was unaware of when I was compiling my study; the last two, in fact, had not yet been published. Pius XII, Paul VI, John Paul II, all three pilgrims to Fatima in different ways, all three admirers of the Portuguese language and culture, will help us to

---

1. Special Preface to the Portuguese edition.

penetrate with greater depth the unique and infinite mystery of both the Virgin and the Church.

Five years after consecrating the world to the Immaculate Heart of Mary, Pius XII, in his letter of May 1, 1947 to a Marian sanctuary in the continent of China, gave us this lapidary declaration: "The bountiful goodness of the Immaculate Heart of Mary is almost infinite, in virtue of that relative infinitude[2] which is, according to the Angelic Doctor,[3] proper to the Mother of God because of her blood relationship to Him."[4] Mary's dignity, "bordering on the infinite" to use St. Thomas Aquinas' daring phrase, came to her because of her divine maternity, through the eternal and infinite Person of the only Son of God. In casting the light of this declaration upon the Immaculate Heart, Pius XII has transfigured the finite, physical, limited, particular character of Mary's created heart through its relationship to the infinitude of the Creator Word, her Son. The heart which at first sight seems very small is thus revealed as an incomprehensible ocean, whose movements and tears, united to those of her Redeemer, expiate the sins of the world which it engulfs and submerges in its cleansing tides. The Heart of Mary, at once physical and spiritual, given its limitations and the infinite will of the Son, acquires a certain spiritual infinitude which is unique in the world of created persons.

Twenty years later, in 1967, Paul VI gave to the entire

---

2. Pius XII, Const. *Novissimo Universorum*: AAS 40 (1948) 492-493. I quote the beautiful Latin text: "Immaculati Mariae Cordis pietas est propemodum infinita ex illa quadam infinitate quam propter consanguineitatem cum Deo Deiparae proprium esse Doctor dicit Angelicus."

3. St. Thomas' expression could be translated: "a quasi infinite dignity." In his text, moreover, he is considering Mary's dignity not only in view of the Incarnation but also of all created happiness (angelic and human) insofar as it is the fruition of God.

4. *Summa Theologiae,* I, 25, 6, 4.

Church the important exhortation *Signum Magnum* on the occasion of his visit to Fatima. In it he draws our attention to "the sweetness and charm emanating from the lofty virtues of the Immaculate Mother of God, which incite souls to imitate Jesus Christ." In fact, "by giving us Mary as our Mother, Jesus has implicitly presented her to us as a model to imitate . . . We all may believe that the divine Savior has left his own Mother to us as a spiritual heritage, together with all the treasures of grace and virtune with which he filled her."[5]

Paul VI was echoing here the exhortation of Vatican Council II "to love this Mother with a filial love and to imitate her virtues."[6]

Such is the fruit of contemplation of the joyful, sorrowful and glorious mysteries of the Rosary. In them we meditate on the virtues of the Mother of God and her Son. In the Rosary, we open ourselves to receive spiritual visits from Mary, who is eager to share with us the virtues of her Immaculate Heart. To recite the Rosary is to let ourselves be invaded by the humility, chastity, patience, joy of Mary, to let her plant in us these firm dispositions, wholly penetrated by supernatural love for her Son and His Church. Through the Rosary the Mother of God comes to us with Him and imprints his image on the altar of our stained hearts. If we place no obstacle to the grace she wishes to obtain for us, we will experience through the Rosary Mary's presence and her transfiguring action. The recitation of the Rosary is thus transformed, if God so wills, into an intimate, mystical experience of the mystery of Mary, making us share at the same time ever more intensely in her virtues. Each of us can then say: "And why is this granted me, that the mother of my Lord should come to me?" (Lk 1:43)

---

5. Paul VI, *Signum Magnum* (SM) AAS 59, 1967, 469 and 473 below.
6. *Lumen Gentium*, No. 67.

These considerations show us the intimate bond existing between the Rosary lived and constantly relived, on the one hand, and on the other, "the avoidance of the double pain of damnation and of the senses, that is to say, the loss of God, our sovereign Good, and the eternal fire." Paul VI, like Mary, evokes this double pain.[7] The Rosary, keeping us far from vice through its cultivation of virtue, makes us share here below in the eternal joy of the God who divinizes us by dwelling in our souls. Through the virtues of Jesus and Mary the divine perfections, residing in the faculties of our souls, dispose us to welcome the grace of final perseverance, which is indispensable if we are to be preserved from the fire of hell. Furthermore, by inciting us to perfect contrition and arousing in us the efficacious desire for a plenary indulgence at the hour of death, these perfections and virtues, cultivated through the Rosary, pave the way for our immediate entrance into heaven without a passage through purgatory.

In helping us to share ever more deeply in the virtues and holiness of the Immaculate Heart of Mary and to contemplate her almost infinite dignity with ever greater love, the Rosary disposes us to understand in depth the original teaching of John Paul II about our personal and individual role in the consecration of the world to this Heart. Since we are the Church, "the Mother of Christ calls upon us to unite ourselves to her in the consecration of the world, and she helps us to do it."[8] The Church which consecrates the world to the Immaculate Heart is not only composed of the pope and bishops who represent us, but also of each one of us, the baptized, in full communion with them. "All is yours, you are Christ's and Mary's, and they are God's" — could we put it this way in connection with Paul's Letter

<hr>

7. *S.M.,* 473.

8. John Paul II, Allocution at Fatima, *Doc. Catholic,* 1982, col. 541.

to the Corinthians? (I Cor. 3:22-23) We refer to his declaration to the Galatians (4:4-5): "God sent forth his Son, born of a woman . . . so that we might receive adoption as sons." Since "all things are ours," thanks to, and with Christ, thanks to the consent of Mary, which procured the filial adoption for us, we should offer this "all," the world, all nations, all cultures, to the Heart of the Mother of Christ who has adopted us in virginally conceiving her only and well-beloved Son.

In other words, the consecration of the world, meaning here Russia and China, would not be complete unless each one of us offers it personally to the Queen of Heaven, thus obtaining from her that each person and each race may ratify this loving oblation in the way appropriate to them.

The missionary thrust of the Portuguese people and their evangelizing role over the last five centuries and more, render them particularly open to perceive what Francisco and Jacinta are contemplating today in the light of glory. The consecration of the world is and remains inseparable from the constant effort to spread everywhere faith in Mary, Mother of the whole Christ, head and members.

Bertrand de Margerie, S.J.,
Paris
May 2, 1991

APPENDIX

MARIAN SUGGESTIONS FOR THE REFORM OF THE LATIN RITE CALENDAR

Changing the Vigil of the Assumption To the Feast of the Dormition of Mary In the Latin Rite

The present liturgy of the Assumption in the Latin rite celebrates Mary's entrance into glory, soul and body. The emphasis is not placed on Mary's death, which Pius XII did not wish to include in the dogmatic definition. He does, however, allude to it in the defining bull, and it is at the least a certain truth taught by the ordinary magisterium of the Church, notably in "her most important organ, the liturgy," to recall the words of Pius XI (see Martimort, *L'Eglise en priere,* Desclee 1961, pp. 221-2).

It would be impossible to underestimate the importance of the numerous witnesses of the Coptic, Byzantine and Latin rites which categorically affirm the death of Mary.

I shall cite the appropriate texts further on.

Since the Church already teaches this truth through her ordinary magisterium and her liturgy, or better, her liturgies, I propose that the present Vigil of the Assumption should be changed into the Feast of the Dormition. The object of the feast would be to celebrate the importance of Mary's death and of her soul's immediate entrance into the beatific vision, for the economy of salvation. The Feast of the Assumption, in contrast, would be the celebration of the Immaculate Virgin's bodily resurrection.

The adoption of the suggested change would, in the Latin rite, transfer the feast of the death or dormition of Mary, "koimesis," which the Coptic rite keeps in January, while celebrating her Assumption, "metastasis," in August. The institution of the Feast of the Dormition in the Latin rite on August 14 would require no calendar change, since it would replace the vigil which now occupies that date, and would be justified by the following reasons and advantages:

1. *On the doctrinal and pedagogical level*: the feast would emphasize a truth that is certain, Mary's death, which has never found adequate expression in the Latin rite, where, since 1950, it has not even been affirmed. The beautiful prayer *Veneranda*, introduced by the Syrian Pope Sergeus I (687-701), has disappeared from the Mass after having proclaimed for twelve centuries the death of Mary.

   The Feast of the Dormition on August 14, by taking this up once more, would explain the meaning of Mary's death in the economy of salvation: her supremely loving and meritorious participation in the death of Jesus and his redemptive sacrifice for humanity. It was the last meritorious action of Mary's sinless liberty, recapitulating all her previous actions. In accepting a death she did not merit, Mary offered her ultimate contribution, I do not say to the objective redemption, but to her own subjective redemption and to that of all humanity. A Feast of the Dormition would be the feast of the subjectively co-redemptive death of Mary, and at the same time of the entrance of her immortal soul into the beatific vision. Celebrated just before the Assumption, and not six months distant as in the Coptic rite (see *Maria*, Vol. VII, p. 177), it would be, together with the Assumption on the following day, like a Marian pendant to the Paschal triduum. Surely it would be odd for us to celebrate only the victorious death of Jesus and to overlook that of his mother, which he merited for her by so great a victory.

What better name could be chosen that that of the Dormition, which is the New Testament designation for the death of the body?

2. *On the ecumenical level*: The institution of the Feast of the Dormition would emphasize, for the Protestant world, the fact that Mary, a creature higher than others, was yet mortal like others, and died as did her Son and Savior. St. John Damascene has already said: "It is not a goddess we are celebrating, like one of the prestigious fables of the Greeks, because we proclaim her death: but we recognize the Mother of the Incarnate God." (PG 96, 743)

3. One objection turns into an additional argument in favor: "Death is tragic and could hardly be the object of feasting." St. John Damascene seems to have foreseen this difficulty. "It is not death which renders you blessed," he says to Mary, "It is you who have illumined death, robbing it of its sadness, and showing us how joy springs out of it" (PG 96, 717c). This obstacle was apparently no hindrance to the Coptic rite ("Hail to the departure of your soul, hail to your death which is like a marriage," concludes the synaxary

of the Assumption (*Maria,* Vol. I, p. 387). Nor did it, for twelve centuries, cause dismay in the Latin rite. "The *festivity* of this day is to be venerated, the day on which the holy Mother of God *underwent* earthly death, yet could not be held by its bonds . . ." We might say then with Father Galot: "Like the death of Christ, [the death of the Mother of God] takes on a higher value, that of a victory over death itself, a triumph of life and joy" (*Maria,* Vol. VII, p. 201).

A Final Note:
Liturgical Texts
On the Death of Mary

The liturgies of the Oriental rites are particularly rich on this theme. I quote, among others, these texts from the Byzantine rite:

"Your death was a passage towards a better and eternal life, O Pure One; from a condition of mortality, it led you to a life which is truly divine and everlasting, O Immaculate One, to the joyful contemplation of your Son and Lord. If her incomprehensible Fruit, thanks to Whom she wins heaven, freely suffers the tomb insofar as He is mortal, how could she refuse this tomb, she who gave birth to Him without the works of marriage?

"It is no marvel that the Virgin, Co-redemptrix of the world, should die, if the Creator of the world Himself died in the flesh."

(Texts cited by Dom Mercenier, *Priere des Eglises du Rite Byzantin*, Amay, 1939, Vol. II, pp. 301, 303; see also pp. 297-299. I do not know whether the work of J. P. O'Connell, *The Testimony of Sacred Liturgy Relative to Mary's Death* in "Marian Studies," 8 (1958), pp. 125-142, makes allusion to Oriental rites.)

N.B. This addition appeared in the review "Ephemerides Mariologicae," Vol. XV (1965) pp. 476-479.

N.B. — On the theme of Mary, Heart of the Church, the reader will find a bibliography in the work of G. Roschini, *Mariologia* (2nd edition, Vol. II, Part II, p. 349 ff.

This work, *Heart of Mary, Heart of the Church*, was originally published in the Review *Ephemerides Mariologicae*, Vol. XVI (1966) pp. 189-227.

More Marian Books and Tapes from the World Apostolate of Fatima

38347   *A SHORT TREATISE ON THE VIRGIN MARY* · By Fr. René Laurentin. Explores doctrinal development of Mary and its scriptural foundation down through the centuries. Each page contains substantial material for study and meditation on Mary. Essential reading for Marian religious communities and lay organizations. 391 pp., paper.. **$14.95**

38608   *PREACHING MARY'S PRAISES* · By Fr. David Q. Liptak. A book to be read, meditated upon and preached. Father Liptak has compiled a series of forty concise and meaningful homilies on the Virgin Mary exploring Marian devotion, her pilgrimage of faith and her example for living the Christian life. 105 pp., paper............ **$ 5.95**

37328   *FATIMA: THE FULL STORY* · by Fr. John DeMarchi, I.M.C. Comprehensive account of Fatima. 256 pp, illus., paper............... **$ 8.25**

37635   *EXPLORING FATIMA* · Explore many exciting aspects of the Fatima message with this fascinating book. Learn the world situation in 1917, study the Fatima children, Mary's role as a catechist and the scriptural meaning of Fatima. 111 pp., paper.............. **$ 4.95**

37362   *FATIMA IN LUCIA'S OWN WORDS* · Outstanding work of Catholic literature. Contains richest, most comprehensive account of Fatima and the apparitions................................ **$ 5.95**

38344   *MARIAN REFLECTIONS* · The Holy Father's Marian teaching from his 1983-1984 Angelus messages edited and with commentary by Servite Fr. David Brown. 150 pp........................... **$ 6.95**

35529   *"THERE IS NOTHING MORE"* · The Rosary, scapular, Immaculate Heart and the Fatima message. 368 pp., paper............ **$ 5.95**

37549   *MEET THE WITNESSES* · by John M. Haffert. Interviews of witnesses of October 13, 1917 solar miracle. 160 pp., illustrated, paper. **$ 3.25**

38195   *BEHOLD YOUR MOTHER: American Bishops' Pastoral Letter* · Concerning authentic Marian devotion. 66 pp., paper.......... **$ 3.75**

38229   *CITY OF GOD* · Detailed life of the Blessed Virgin by Mary of Agreda. 4 volumes, 2676 pp., hardcover...................... **$49.00**

38390   *SERMONS OF ST. FRANCIS DE SALES ON OUR LADY* · Marian teachings from a saint and doctor of the Church. 219 pp., paper.. **$ 9.00**

38518   *TRUE DEVOTION TO MARY* · by St. Louis Grignion de Montfort. A classical masterpiece on true devotion, showing the need to go to Jesus through Mary. 85 pp., paper........................ **$ 4.50**

38607   *MARY OF NAZARETH AND THE HIDDEN LIFE OF JESUS* · by Msgr. Eugene Kevane. Explores life of Jesus and Mary at Nazareth based on Scripture and revolutionary new Jewish scholarship on Jesus.. **$ 1.95**

38609   *CATECHESIS: THE MISSION OF THE WORLD APOSTOLATE OF FATIMA* · by Fr. John A. Hardon, S.J. Fr. Hardon's thought-provoking discussion of what is perhaps the most important aspect of the Fatima message. 16 pp., paper.......................... **$ .50**

| 38611 | ***MARY: CATECHIST AT FATIMA*** - by Fr. Frederick L. Miller. The apparitions of Fatima are viewed in a new light in this booklet, which highlights a dimension of Fatima all but ignored for the past seventy years. Excellent for those involved in catechetical work. | $ 1.50 |

| 49734 | ***MARY AND THE PRIESTHOOD*** - By Frederick L. Miller. Mary's indispensable place in the life of every seminarian and priest.... | $ 1.95 |

| 39400 | ***THE "CREDO" OF THE PEOPLE OF GOD*** - by Pope Paul VI. Comprehensive summation of the Catholic Faith................. | $ .50 |

| 40983 | ***17 PAPAL DOCUMENTS ON THE ROSARY*** - Contains *Marialis Cultis*. Superb reference. 150 pp., paper....................... | $ 2.50 |

| 51313 | ***BROWN SCAPULAR OF MOUNT CARMEL*** - by Fr. Barry Bossa, S.A.C. Illustrated history. 50 pp., paper..................... | $ 2.50 |

| 42045 | ***ISIDORE BAKANJA — Africa's Scapular Martyr*** - by Fr. Redemptus M. Valabek, O.Carm. True story about a young man who suffered martyrdom rather than renounce his Christian beliefs. 19 pp., paper... | $ 1.75 |

| 42739 | ***CATHOLICISM & FUNDAMENTALISM*** - by Karl Keating. Covers all key issues of Catholic-"Bible Christian" clash. Proves Catholic position via the Bible, early Christian writers and plain common sense. 360 pp., paper................................... | $12.95 |

| 48589 | ***A HANDBOOK OF PRAYERS*** - A complete treasury of prayers and Latin-English order of Mass. Pocket-size prayer book to carry with you. 376 pp., vinyl...................................... | $11.95 |

Audio Tapes

| 361920 | ***Fatima in Perspective*** This wonderful five-tape album takes you to the Jubilee Year National Fatima Conference at the Shrine of the Immaculate Heart of Mary. Features: *Fatima and Communism; The Crisis in Contemporary Catechetics; Fatima and the Antichrist; Mary at Fatima – Image and Model of the Church in the 21st Century* and *The Mission of Women*.................. | $19.95 |

| 362500 | ***Fatima and the Modern World*** by Fr. John A. Hardon, S.J. This five-tape series includes *Fatima and Miracles of Conversion; Fatima and the Papal Primacy; Fatima and Heroic Chastity; Fatima and the Age of Martyrs* and *Fatima and the Pro-Life Movement*. Each presentation approx. 60 min............................. | $19.95 |

| 361572 | ***Formation in the Fatima Message.*** Presentations on formation in the Fatima message and the catechetical truths of Fatima by Fr. Frederick L. Miller and Fatima Sanctuary Rector Msgr. Luciano Guerra answering questions about Fatima. A four-tape series.. | $17.00 |

| 361574 | ***Mary in Scripture and in the Teaching of the Church*** by Fr. Frederick L. Miller. This five-tape series includes presentations on the mystery of Mary and the Immaculate Conception, her perpetual virginity, divine maternity and her role as model of the Church. A five-tape series... | $19.95 |

| 361576 | ***The Christian Woman in the Modern World*** by Dr. Alice von Hildebrand. Features presentations on the life of Edith Stein, the role of women in the Church and the virtue of purity. A five-tape series. | $19.95 |

| 361912 | ***Fatima and America.*** Five-cassette album featuring: *Living the Fatima Message* by Fr. John A. Hardon, S.J.; *Fatima and the Church in America* by Bishop Austin B. Vaughan; *Fatima and the Church's Moral Teaching* by Fr. Anthony Mastroeni and *Fatima and Modernism* by Fr. Robert I. Bradley, S.J....................... | $19.95 |

361915 ***Exploring Fatima.*** Explore many exciting aspects of the Fatima message with this six-cassette album. Learn the world situation in 1917, study the Fatima children, Mary's role as a catechist and the scriptural meaning of Fatima............................ **$21.95**

361916 ***Fatima Today!*** Six-cassette album featuring *The Fatima Message in the Modern World*; *The Masonic Movement and the Fatima Message*; *Fatima and Recent Developments in Russia* and *The 1984 Consecration of Pope John Paul II*.......................... **$21.95**

362745 ***Mother Teresa*** speaks to pilgrims at the Shrine of the Immaculate Heart of Mary. On side 2, Fr. Frederick Miller talks on Total Consecration to Jesus through Mary............................ **$ 4.95**

361564 ***Mary in the Scriptures*** by Msgr. James C. Turro............. **$ 4.95**

361569 ***True Devotion to Mary*** by Sr. Mary Frederick, M.C............ **$ 4.95**

361578 ***Catechesis: The Mission/Mother of Sorrows*** by Fr. John A. Hardon, S.J. This cassette covers two talks given by Jesuit Fr. John A. Hardon to World Apostolate of Fatima leaders in September, 1990... **$ 4.95**

361914 ***St. Joseph in the Teaching of Pope John Paul II*** by Fr. Frederick L. Miller. Explores the special relationship of St. Joseph to Jesus and Mary and his role in the Redemption as taught by Pope John Paul II.. **$ 4.95**

NAME_____

STREET_____

CITY_____

STATE_____ ZIP_____

**World Apostolate
of Fatima**
P.O. Box 976
Washington,
NJ 07882-0976
(908) 689-1700

Qty.	Item #	Title/Description	Price Each	Total Price	

Please add proper shipping and handling
charge shown below

Value of Order	USA	Foreign
$.00 – $1.99	$1.05	Customers
$2.00 – $24.99	$3.45	will be
$25.00 – $49.99	$5.25	billed
$50.00 – $99.99	$7.55	for
Over $100	Add 15%	postage.

Subtotal		
N.J. residents: Add state sales tax		
Shipping & Handling		
Donation		
Total*		

Please make checks payable to:
World Apostolate of Fatima
* U.S. funds payable through a U.S. bank.
Postal money orders in U.S. funds are accepted.
Prices subject to change without notice

Heart of Mary
Heart of Church